HOME

edited by christian wiman

home

100 poems

Yale UNIVERSITY PRESS NEW HAVEN AND LONDON

Published with support from the Fund established in memory of Oliver Baty Cunningham, a distinguished graduate of the Class of 1917, Yale College, Captain, 15th United States Field Artillery, born in Chicago September 17, 1894, and killed while on active duty near Thiaucourt, France, September 17, 1918, the twenty-fourth anniversary of his birth.

Yale University Press books may be purchased in quantity for educational, business, or promotional use. For information, please email sales.press@yale.edu (U.S. office) or sales@yaleup.co.uk (U.K. office).

Set in The Sans & Sabon type by INTEGRATED PUBLISHING SOLUTIONS, GRAND RAPIDS, MICHIGAN. Printed in the United States of America.

Library of Congress Control Number: 2021938290
ISBN 978-0-300-25345-0 (hardcover : alk. paper)

A catalogue record for this book is available from the British Library.

This paper meets the requirements of ANSI/NISO Z39.48-1992 (Permanence of Paper).

10 9 8 7 6 5 4 3 2 1

CONTENTS

INTERLUDES

Like its predecessor (*Joy: 100 Poems*), this anthology includes a number of quotations from other texts, which are intended to inflect individual poems or groups of poems in different ways. Some of the quotations contradict each other and/or points I have made in my introduction. As with *Joy*, this seems inevitable and necessary for any book that is not meant to be an argument, but an experience.

I.

A few years ago I edited an anthology of poems called *Joy*. I intended this new anthology to be a companion book, and in many ways—historical parameters, variety of voices, even the combination of poetry and prose—it is. But in one major way it's not. In *Joy*, a long and wide-ranging search led me to an increasingly focused sense of what the word might mean. With *Home*, a similar search has caused the governing word to disperse into more definitions than one book can contain. This frustrated me for a while. A word that means everything—home is a house, a country, a language, a love, a longing, a grief, a god—means nothing. Gradually, though, I have found the linguistic slippage provocative. A word whose meanings are so various and contradictory means something is deeply—and still—at stake. A certain circularity is to be expected—and not embraced, either, but endured. "In the realm of primal words," as Josef Pieper says, "we are always on the verge of tautology."

Poetry, though, can push thought beyond tautology. "I have learned and dismantled all the words," writes Mahmoud Darwish, "in order to draw from them a single word: *Home*." Note the progression: first he learned, then he dismantled. First he carefully assembled a structure adequate to his love and longing, then he suffered its destruction to get back to some original source. As with other primal words—*poetry* is one, actually—the cost of knowledge is loss.

Darwish was Palestinian (he died in 2008) and often linked the past of that place to Eden. But as both the quotation and the mythologizing impulse suggest, an existential homelessness preceded the political one. To be a poet is to be an exile. ("All poets are Jews," said Marina Tsvetaeva provocatively.) Or rather, one doesn't become a poet unless one senses (suffers) the aboriginal exile that is consciousness. This happens early on, maybe in a home that isn't one, perhaps, or a home that, though entirely protective and enveloping, nevertheless disquiets somehow, or can't quite include the consciousness that has come to inhabit it. Poets are those whose souls will not let them keep this disquiet quiet. But this is ultimately a difference of degree and not of kind. Eventually, for everyone, in every home no matter how secure, that little drone in the distance—that drone that *is* distance—becomes a roar.

> who told you you could settle in?
> who told you this or that would last forever?
> didn't anyone tell you you'll never
> in the world
> feel at home here?

STANISŁAW BARAŃCZAK, "IF CHINA"
(TRANSLATED FROM THE POLISH
BY MAGNUS J. KRYNSKI)

But someone did tell us, didn't they? Existence whispered in our ear at some point, with or without words, for each of us knows, even if we have never *known,* that pull toward "a place of first permission," as Robert Duncan put it, some time so replete with being it seems timeless, wordless, "everlasting omen of what is." Certainly Barańczak's poem suggests such knowledge. Its conclusion is less question than cry, and the syntax makes that cry cosmic: "you'll never / *in the world* / feel at home here." Yet if there is no such thing as a true home for us in this world, how is it that we have such a strong sense for what it is? For that's the other thing to note in the Darwish quote. The cost of knowledge may be loss, but some definite-but-not-quite-definable gain radiates through the space cleared by that loss. Maybe home, for us moderns, is like time for ancient Augustine: We know what it means, we know it intimately, utterly, in the very cells and silences of our bones—just as long as you don't ask us.

2.

An earlier version of this book began with Emily Dickinson and ended with Walt Whitman. It's so easy to plot consciousness between them. The acetylene burn of single being versus the dispersal of ecstatic union. The home that is so self-contained, its daily details so fraught and lit with eternity, that one need never leave the yard ("Never for Society/He shall seek in vain—/Who His own acquaintance/Cultivate"), against the kind of life in which the notion of home is so peripatetic, fluid, and expansive that its apotheosis is simply the random atoms into which the body dissolves ("If you want me again look for me under your bootsoles"). Stasis and kinesis, focus and scope, home and homeland.

Too easy, in the end. And too American. "As you set out for Ithaka/hope your road is a long one," writes Constantine Cavafy; hope, that is, that the longing that sets you searching is never answered, or answered only insofar as the experiences along the way are intensified by their very insufficiency; hope, in other words, that hope itself becomes your home. "We will rise again beneath the walls of Knossos" is Sophia de Mello Breyner Andresen's answer, "And in Delphi the centre of the world/We will rise again in the harsh light of Crete." Her poem concludes:

For it is good to clarify the heart of man
And to lift the black exactness of the cross
In the white light of Crete

TRANSLATED FROM THE PORTUGUESE

BY RICHARD ZENITH

Forget, for now, the specifically religious dimension of this poem and simply note the hard lines, the "black exactness" of place and pain that clearly counter the restless hunger of Cavafy's poem. This tension between diffusion and concentration, roaming and rootedness, home as a place and home as a state of mind, is everywhere in this book, often in the same poem.

3.

"The only home is memory," writes Terry Tempest Williams. Is that true? To some extent. Barring some dire trauma, which can scorch even the Eden of pre-consciousness, and excepting for the meteoric but probably hyperbolic outlier (Osip Mandelstam: "My memory is inimical to all that is personal"), it's likely that any notion of home we have is also a matter of memory. Perhaps there really was a time when humans were, as Eric A. Havelock argues of "Homeric man," so rooted in timeless life, so much "a part of all [they] had seen and heard and remembered," that their existence was essentially a "surrender accomplished through the lavish employment of the emotions and of the motor reflexes." But we have eaten of the bread of Augustine, Hegel, Freud. Our lives are constructed, as are our homes. We build them out of homes we've known, even if our efforts are reactive.

Home
A road ran
past our house. I
ran faster.

ANDREA COHEN

Since Romanticism, and William Wordsworth in particular (to whom Freud expressed a debt), most people have assumed some ultimate source of self and home in childhood. I have done so myself in things I have written, even though I don't think we've somehow discovered *the* truth about this aspect of human consciousness. It is *a* truth, and like most truths, it can become inert if uncontested.

Nostos
There was an apple tree in the yard—
this would have been
forty years ago—behind,
only meadows. Drifts
of crocus in the damp grass.
I stood at that window:
late April. Spring
flowers in the neighbor's yard.
How many times, really, did the tree
flower on my birthday,
the exact day, not
before, not after? Substitution
of the immutable
for the shifting, the evolving.
Substitution of the image
for relentless earth. What
do I know of this place,
the role of the tree for decades
taken by a bonsai, voices
rising from the tennis courts—
Fields. Smell of the tall grass, new cut.
As one expects of a lyric poet.
We look at the world once, in childhood.
The rest is memory.

LOUISE GLÜCK

You wouldn't say the nostalgia of this vision is uncontested. It's given an acid bath in irony. ("Nostos" is Greek for homecoming, specifically a heroic one.) But it's still nostalgia; it still locates, and grieves for, some meaning and being that are sealed in an unrecoverable past. In essence it's Romanticism minus the joy. Wordsworth believed childhood was a time of spiritual permeability and intensity compared to which adult existence was a pale shadow. But he also believed that the mind and the world, in some primary way, rhymed. To become aware of this could lead to what the philosopher Richard Kearney, in a different context, calls "sacramental sensation," which is "a reversible rapport between myself and things, wherein the sensible gives birth to itself through me." What this means practically is that memory might not simply be occasioned by the physical world— a madeleine, say—but actually inhere within it. What it means existentially is that life is not some linear frog-march between pure being and pure oblivion; the past isn't inert and sealed off but volatile, available, even salvific:

> O joy! that in our embers
> Is something that doth live,
> That Nature yet remembers
> What was so fugitive!
> The thought of our past years in me doth breed
> Perpetual benediction: not indeed
> For that which is most worthy to be blest;
> Delight and liberty, the simple creed
> Of Childhood, whether busy or at rest,
> With new-fledged hope still fluttering in his breast:—
> Not for these I raise
> The song of thanks and praise
> But for those obstinate questionings

Of sense and outward things,
Fallings from us, vanishings;
Blank misgivings of a Creature
Moving about in worlds not realised,
High instincts before which our mortal Nature
Did tremble like a guilty thing surprised:
But for those first affections,
Those shadowy recollections,
Which, be they what they may
Are yet the fountain-light of all our day,
Are yet a master-light of all our seeing;
Uphold us, cherish, and have power to make
Our noisy years seem moments in the being
Of the eternal Silence.

WILLIAM WORDSWORTH, "ODE:
INTIMATIONS OF IMMORTALITY"

Granted, this kind of confidence is probably *not* available to us, and I have singled out Glück's poem partly because I have sympathy for, and resonance with, her bitter vision. I also find the extreme self-consciousness ("As one expects of a lyric poet") chastening given the tendency of so much modern poetry (especially American poetry, especially American men's poetry) to be too automatically elegiac, too self-pleasuringly sorrowful, about the past—all those "triggering towns" where "women cluck like starved pullets" and everything is ambered in bourbon. But I do find Glück's vision limited and limiting, and the poems I have gravitated toward for this book tend to be, in terms of memory and home, more enlivened (and abraded) by the possibility of revelation, communication, joy. "Memory is a strange bell," as Dickinson says, "Both Jubilee and Knell."

4.

A related note: I have found few poems of direct, uncomplicated domestic fulfillment. A sense of home not fraught with actual or impending loss. "Every single minute brings someone closer to something he will not be able to bear," writes Simone Weil. Setting aside the random sociopath who dies quietly in his sleep, the point is hard to argue. One waters one's plants and sets out the doily, one "arranges the rows of cans/so that they softly say:/ESSO—SO—SO—SO," but always there is that distant roar.

The Niagara River
As though
the river were
a floor, we position
our table and chairs
upon it, eat, and
have conversation.
As it moves along,
we notice—as
calmly as though
dining room paintings
were being replaced—
the changing scenes
along the shore. We
do know, we do
know this is the
Niagara River, but
it is hard to remember
what that means.

KAY RYAN

What that means is an end to everything we have and love, the whole kit and caboodle of our carefully constructed lives crashing down some Niagara of intake forms, formaldehyde, and tag sales, oblivion swallowing it all down without so much as a burp. This undertow, the tick-tock mortality of poetry (of life), the sense that even our joys come to us through a scrim of sorrow and longing, can be oppressive if it's all you learn to hear.

But there's an interesting paradox in this poem: we must *remember* what is ahead of us, as if our deaths were in our past. ("Our birth is but a sleep and a forgetting," as Wordsworth says.) Another interesting thing: time as a river is a common metaphor, in which there is never a now one can seize and hold. Rivers run toward seas, though (in this instance an immense lake, but close enough); implicit within the image is a much larger life with which the one river eventually merges. "People still persist in thinking that *life is flat*," wrote Vincent van Gogh, "and runs from birth to death. But life, too, is probably round, and much greater in scope and possibilities than the hemisphere we now know." I find that a powerful intellectual consolation but a difficult thing to genuinely feel—except in certain moments. Poems can be such moments. Certainly this poem by Kay Ryan, with its two undertows, is that for me. It momentarily transcends the limitations to which it seems to concede. It briefly releases a reader from the confinement it describes as absolute.

5.

And here I'm approaching an idea that recurs repeatedly among modern people, the notion that art itself can be a home, or at least the surest way toward it.

Only in the most

Careful details of the most extreme
Philosophies, the most careful stones
Of the breathless cathedrals, the claims

Of the most elaborate musics
On our souls do we start to dissolve
As though we had a home, and lived there.

VICKI HEARNE, "ON R.L.S.

AND HAPPINESS"

As though. Hearne was too rigorous a philosopher to make the
equation complete. Other modern artists have not been so profes-
sionally reticent. Wassily Kandinsky believed an invisible reality
underlay every detail of the one we see. World is not world so long
as it's merely that. "The world sounds," he wrote. "It is a cosmos
of spiritually affective beings. Thus dead matter is living spirit." He
believed abstract art capable of making—or bringing forth, really—
this "sound." In his book on Kandinsky, *Seeing the Invisible,* the
philosopher Michel Henry goes a step further: "Because art brings
about the revelation of invisible reality in us, and with absolute
certainty, it constitutes salvation and, in a society like our own,
which disregards life . . . it is the only salvation possible." Once
more my reaction is mixed. I find this intellectually provocative
and spiritually dampening. Piercingly accurate and entirely wrong.
(The *only* salvation possible?) And once more the vertigo inspired
by thinking about art (and God) is only relieved by the real thing.

Bassey the bassist
loves his lady

hugs her to him
like a baby

plucks her
chucks her

makes her
boom

waltz or tango
bop or shango

watch them walk
or do the 'dango:

bassey and his lovely lady

bassey and his lovely lady
like the light and not the shady:

bit by boom
they build from duty

humming strings and throbbing
beauty:

beat by boom
they build this beauty:

bassey and his lovely lady

KAMAU BRATHWAITE, "BLUES"

There is no "lady" in this poem. There is nothing being built. Yet
one feels (I feel) a great loneliness eased and some kind of untouch-
able (but reachable) shelter in the sound. *Feels* is the operative word.
Perhaps the key to these quotations that have given me both provo-

cation and pause lies back in the fourteenth century: "By love he may be gotten and holden; but by thought, never." The anonymous author of that quotation from *The Cloud of Unknowing* is referring to God, but he might have been referring to home (or joy, or love, or art) as well.

6.

Best of any song
is bird song
in the quiet, but first
you must have the quiet.

WENDELL BERRY, *A Timbered Choir:*
The Sabbath Poems, 1979–1997

Enough abstractions, then. Home may be hard to define, but it is primarily, blessedly, relentlessly physical. (Whitman's intuition of his afterlife in the dirt beneath someone's boots is, to my mind, entirely congruent with Wordsworth's prenatal Heaven.) In fact, any idea of home that is not first physical is not only doomed; it is itself both engine and agent of that doom.

Even while I dreamed I prayed that what I saw was only fear
 and no foretelling,
for I saw the last known landscape destroyed for the sake
of the objective, the soil bulldozed, the rock blasted.
Those who had wanted to go home would never get there
 now.

That's from the same poem as the birdsong that emerges out of—and cedes to—primal silence. It's the longest poem in this book and is at once lyric, love poem, elegy, ode, and jeremiad. It's also an incandescent exception to the rule of ambivalence about home. Berry has famously staked his claim (and life) to one place in Kentucky which his descendants have loved (and plundered: he faces this fact squarely) for centuries. Describing how his attention has been honed, and his feeling for people, language, and the physical world deepened and sacralized, he says, "I had made a significant change in my relation to the place; before, it had been mine by coincidence or accident; now it was mine by choice." (I am reminded of Paul Ricoeur's definition of his own Christian faith as "chance turned into destiny by virtue of a constant choice.") That freedom of full commitment enables not only love, but also a lucid and liberating grief.

> "You see," my mother said, and laughed,
> knowing I knew the passage
> she was remembering, "finally you lose
> everything."

What passage? The poem never says. The lost words—the stamp of *meaning* they suggest—become birds, which become flowers, which become the blue sky. Ordinary details of an ordinary day, though all of it so lit with the "inextinguishable delight" the mother took in the world and has now bequeathed to the son that he is freed not only to grieve her death, but also, on the next page, for this:

> The lovers know the loveliness
> That is not of their bodies only
> (Though they be lovely) but is of
> Their bodies given up to love.
>
> They find the open-heartedness
> Of two desires which both are lonely

Until by dying they have their living,
And gain all they have lost in giving,

Each offering the desired desire.
Beyond what time requires, they are
What they surpass themselves to make;
They give the pleasure that they take.

7.

But some people don't get such a choice. Some people are driven
from their homes by force or disaster, are imprisoned or impover-
ished, or have demons in their heads who are disinclined to heed
their host's "choice." Some souls are so displaced that place itself
becomes a gall to them. Home, if it exists at all, is some hard and
buried sphere of soul that one seeks only to keep intact, while the
self scurries around on the burning surface trying to survive.

Balance
He watch her like a coonhound watch a tree.
What might explain the metamorphosis
he underwent when she paraded by
with tea-cakes, in her fresh and shabby dress?
(As one would carry water from a well—
straight-backed, high-headed, like a diadem,
with careful grace so that no drop will spill—
she balanced, almost brimming, her one name.)

She think she something, stuck-up island bitch.
Chopping wood, hanging laundry on the line,
and tantalizingly within his reach,
she honed his body's yearning to a keen,

sharp point. And on that point she balanced life.
That hoe Diverne think she Marse Tyler's wife.

I have been reading and teaching this poem for thirty years and am
still shocked by its terrible perfections: the "balance" between the
powerlessness of Diverne—who is twice displaced, alien both to the
white life of the plantation and to the other slaves—and the "power"
she wields with her body; between the language of slaves and that
of the educated poet who is descended from them; between evil so
infernal its embers still smolder in our streets today—

Ours is a country in which a boy shot by police lies on the pavement
for hours.

We see in his open mouth
the nakedness
of the whole nation.

ILYA KAMINSKY,
"IN A TIME OF PEACE"

—and the singular, wily, willful, triumphant life emerging from
it. Because make no mistake: this small poem is a large triumph.
Diverne, who is quite real (see Nelson's *The Homeplace*), survives,
as do the children who emerge out of this ambiguous union, as does
the feeling they and their descendants have that Marse Tyler, too, is
part of their past, their place, their family, their "home."

History reveals its essence only to those it excludes. That's the
conclusion drawn by László F. Földényi in an essay speculating
that Dostoevsky, exiled and imprisoned in Siberia, might have read
Hegel's lectures on the completely rational arrangement of world

history, specifically a brief passage in which he lops off Siberia and Africa as irrelevant to his ideas because no history had happened there. Dostoevsky, to whom history still seemed to be very much happening, who could in fact feel its irrational lashes on his flesh, might have been, Földényi suggests, not simply appalled but propelled into the ideas animating his later work.

> It becomes necessary . . . to accept the possibility of a *miracle*—that state at which the exclusivity of space and time ceases. And if Hegel permits continent-sized chunks of land to become detached from history, it means that history itself does not contain within itself divine boundlessness: there is yet something that surrounds history which is beyond it. Namely: what is necessary will be contiguous with what is impossible, what is natural will be contiguous with the arbitrary, politics will be contiguous with theology. And yet what is beyond the borders is always seeping through the borders, to within.

History, then, can't explain all dimensions of human experience. To become conscious of this doesn't lead to an end of suffering; it might, in terms of loneliness, momentarily increase it. But it might also lead to genuine enlightenment and even "a kind of redemption—namely, an inner balance [!], an inner healthiness—instead of suffocating and undermining a person from inside."

8.

What is the right relationship of security to precarity? Between those who have (literal) homes and those who don't? How should the man or woman sitting in the sunlit backyard, sipping gin and watching the children play, relate to the Syrian child photographed bloated and face-down on a beach in Turkey (2015), or to the half-million US citizens who on any given night are homeless, or to George Floyd, Breonna Taylor, Stephon Clark, Philando Castile, Tamir Rice, Michael Brown, Eric Garner (how insidious the etcetera one is forced into at some point). Primo Levi has an answer.

Shema
You who live secure
In your warm houses
Who return at evening to find
Hot food and friendly faces:

> Consider whether this is a man,
> Who labours in the mud
> Who knows no peace
> Who fights for a crust of bread
> Who dies at a yes or a no.
> Consider whether this is a woman,
> Without hair or name
> With no more strength to remember
> Eyes empty and womb cold
> As a frog in winter.

Consider that this has been:
I commend these words to you.
Engrave them on your hearts
When you are in your house, when you walk on your way,
When you go to bed, when you rise.
Repeat them to your children.
Or may your house crumble,
Disease render you powerless,
Your offspring avert their faces from you.

TRANSLATED FROM THE ITALIAN
BY RUTH FELDMAN AND BRIAN SWANN

The shema, in Jewish tradition, is a liturgical prayer derived from verses in Deuteronomy and Numbers. It amounts to a confession of faith and is to be recited every morning and evening of the devout person's life. The shema, in this poem, is an anti-prayer, less a pledge of faith than a promise to haunt. It asks (demands, really) that certain forms of human suffering be so inscribed on the hearts of those who have not known them that there be no oblivion powerful enough to erase the fact of their having been. Levi placed this poem at the beginning of his memoir of Auschwitz, *If This Is a Man,* which also contains this searing passage:

> Auschwitz is outside of us, but it is all around us, in the air. The plague has died away, but the infection still lingers and it would be foolish to deny it. Rejection of human solidarity, obtuse and cynical indifference to the suffering of others, abdication of the intellect and of moral sense to the principle of authority, and above all, at the root of everything, a sweeping tide of cowardice, a colossal cowardice which masks itself as warring virtue, love of country and faith in an idea.

How does Wendell Berry's poem of domestic tranquility hold up against Levi's invective? Berry's poem, after all, is very much about virtue, love of country, and faith in an idea. But none of this is a mask in Berry. Not only is the poem bitterly and tenderly conscious of human suffering, but the very way in which its final truth is articulated underscores its existential diffidence.

> There is a day
> when the road neither
> comes nor goes, and the way
> is not a way but a place.

This is such a rocklike utterance, feels so arrived-at and earned and durable, that you hardly notice the evanescence it suggests. To say "there is a day" implies an otherwise. There are a lot of restless yesterdays behind these lines and, inevitably, some dark tomorrow. (Think how differently the poem would read if the line was "There is a time.") It's as if Berry has built one of those momentary architectural marvels made entirely out of the landscape into which, like a life well lived, it eventually disappears.

The circle of responsibility is larger than the circle of guilt. The former includes, even for the man or woman sitting outside sipping gin, Auschwitz, and the trans-Atlantic slave trade, and the next Texas-sized mass of ice lopped off the Arctic. We are attuned to, mingled with, even dependent on, forms of existence that seem alien to us. We owe a debt to deaths we never know. This doesn't mean one need brood over human misery like some backyard flagellant. Peace is not something for which we need forgiveness, unless it's tainted with pure forgetfulness (you "forget that you have forgotten," as Berry says), the cold morphine of *mine*. But should a certain defensiveness creep in, should you find yourself wondering what a strangled Black man or a drowned migrant have to do with you, then it's time to say the shema.

9.

> With all its eyes the natural world looks out
> into the Open. Only *our* eyes are turned
> backward, and surround plant, animal, child
> like traps, as they emerge into their freedom.
> We know what is really out there only from
> the animal's gaze; for we take the very young

child and force it around, so that it sees
objects—not the Open, which is so
deep in animals' faces. Free from death.

That's Rilke in the "Eighth Elegy," a poem I find (like Rilke in
general) both illuminating and frustrating, elusive and true. First, the
truth. We live adjacent to things. There is some posture of departure
inherent in our being. The cost of knowledge is loss.

And yet this is not the entire truth. We are not as separate from
nature as this poem suggests. We too are made of matter, and I've
known dogs who knew more about death than some people. ("Dogs
are in general more skilled at belief than we are"—Vicki Hearne.)
There are minds, and there are moments, that do in fact "have before
[them] that pure space into which flowers endlessly open." There
are clearings we come into that really are a "Nowhere without the
No." It's lovely the spiritual clarities that Rilke—and the translator,
Stephen Mitchell—manage in both of these instances. You almost
feel the freedom you're being denied.

"It is an elegant paradox," says Kay Ryan, "that an accurate de-
scription of the physical world frees us from it." As Rilke's poem
shows, this can happen with abstractions too. But a couple of ques-
tions nag. First, *why* should such linguistic accuracy bring such
release? Because it is not mere accuracy but intimacy, perhaps?
Because there is in fact some connection between reality and the
language we use to inhabit it? "There are things we live among,"
writes George Oppen, "and to know them/is to know ourselves."
Is it possible that when Czesław Miłosz says that "language is our
only homeland" and Francis Ponge says "the silent world is our only
homeland," they are, in fact, in complete agreement?

The second question that arises from Ryan's perception, though (and that speaks directly to the Rilke poem), is what exactly such accuracy/intimacy frees us *for*. What we are freed *from* is clear enough: our alienation from nature, our tick-tock mortality, the oppressive linearity of that damn river. But what does such a moment free us *for*? If the answer is nothing, if this momentary clarity is entirely self-contained, then poetry (all art) is little more than diversion and illusion. The claims made for art by Kandinsky, and even more so by Michel Henry, are absurd. Poems are simply "machines for the suppression of time," as Claude Lévi-Strauss said of both myths and music.

I don't buy it. I believe that Marilyn Nelson's "Balance" is in fact a miracle in the old-fashioned metaphysical sense of the term. Something in her mind and something deep in time merged—and saved both. When Atsuro Riley conjures out of sound a drain-pipe big enough for a small child to crawl inside, and a child lonely enough to stay there, and shapes and shades that reach from rural Alabama back to Plato's cave, one feels a whole life has been rescued from whatever terrors—the poem implies that there were some—made him seek such shelter in the first place.

What the boy called inside-*oku* called him back. He was hooked right quick on the well-bottom peace of the pumicey concrete and how sounds sounded in there, and re-sounded. Tight-curled as he had to get—like a cling-shrimp one day, a pill-bug, a bass-clef, a bison's eye; an abalone (*ocean-ear!*), antler-arc, Ark-ant, apostrophe another— sure as clocks a cool clear under-creek would rise, and rinse him through, and runnel free. Hanging in a green-pine O outside were sun-heat and smaze and BB-fire and Mosquito Abatement. Inside there were water-limber words (and a picture-noisy nave), shades of shade.

ATSURO RILEY, "FLINT-CHANT"

Sure as clocks, that's how Riley describes the sound the boy learns to make in this cast-off drainpipe in Alabama, this little "Nowhere without the No." I don't know if the grown poet still carries this saving space in his own soul. But I know at least one reader who has.

Robert Frost famously defined poetry as "a momentary stay against confusion." It's certainly that. But it's also a momentary stay *for* confusion. Not the confusion of complete chaos, but the confusion of complete being. Wonder is a truer word.

> **The Bennett Springs Road**
> I knew it was there, if I'd had time to look:
> the sweet water falling over rock,
> the leaf-mold floor, secret to all but light,
> the tall boles stationed between day and night.
>
> This is the heart of the mountain, not the crest.
> Season and century league in some high place,
> impulsive powers that beat the peak to sand
> and scatter Appalachian on the wind.
>
> And lie at last by the little stream that brings
> all gods to truth. On the road to Bennett Springs,
> tired of the paltry ridges, I lay down
> the last of my youth where all the gods had grown,
> became the water falling over the stone,
> became the forest-father to red men,
> became the tribe of stars, both daughter and son,
> the mother of moss, the bird that sang I am.
>
> JULIA RANDALL

10.

That is a very natural place to end this essay. At the "heart of the mountain, not the crest"; beside "the little stream that brings/all gods to truth"; and with a bird that "sings very close to the music of what happens" (Seamus Heaney) and the music of what happens is exactly as clear, exactly as incomprehensible, as the ongoingness of God ("I am that I am").

But I am writing in an unnatural time. I decided to turn my attention to the idea of home just when fate decided to confine me to a literal one. This book was completed entirely in quarantine, and though there are no poems that specifically mention that misery, its influence is everywhere. In the selections, first of all, since I have had no access to a library and couldn't read as systematically as I have in the past. But also in the urgency the word acquired for me. If it's true that only those who lose a home know what one is, in recent months many of us have learned a burning corollary: nothing tests one's attachment to home like being confined to it.

Misery? Certainly there has been some. The loneliness of not seeing friends and family, the spiritual withering caused by the wrong solitudes, the collective domestic irritations that accumulate in a closed house like an infestation.

But that's hardly the whole story. I have a huge hillbilly pool smack dab in my driveway. And two eleven-year-old girls who have grown inches and eons since the door to our house shut. And a new pup, a little volt of soul named Rosie who was rescued, at four weeks and four pounds, trawling through trash in Georgia. I have a study half-filled floor to ceiling with *disjecta membra* from this project that, as Paul Valéry said of a poem—and as seems to me true of a home—can never be finished, only abandoned.

Why this personal note in this most impersonal of books? Because "one only reads well what one reads with some quite personal purpose" (Valéry again). And because in a land of masks, certain kinds of candor matter more than ever. And because, amid the miseries of separation and isolation, and though my life has been somewhat frantically nomadic, there are still days when chance and choice can coincide, and I look up from my work to hear a sudden splash of laughter and a pup's companionable yaps, and the way is not a way but a place.

HOME

I BELONG THERE

I belong there. I have many memories. I was born as everyone is
   born.
I have a mother, a house with many windows, brothers, friends, and
   a prison cell
with a chilly window! I have a wave snatched by seagulls, a
   panorama of my own.
I have a saturated meadow. In the deep horizon of my word, I have a
   moon,
a bird's sustenance, and an immortal olive tree.
I have lived on the land long before swords turned man into prey.
I belong there. When heaven mourns for her mother, I return heaven
   to her mother.
And I cry so that a returning cloud might carry my tears.
To break the rules, I have learned all the words needed for a trial by
   blood.
I have learned and dismantled all the words in order to draw from
   them a single word: *Home.*

MAHMOUD DARWISH

(TRANSLATED FROM THE ARABIC BY

MUNIR AKASH AND CAROLYN FORCHÉ)

MY DREAMS, MY WORKS, MUST WAIT TILL AFTER HELL

I hold my honey and I store my bread
In little jars and cabinets of my will.
I label clearly, and each latch and lid
I bid, Be firm till I return from hell.
I am very hungry. I am incomplete.
And none can tell when I may dine again.
No man can give me any word but Wait,
The puny light. I keep eyes pointed in;
Hoping that, when the devil days of my hurt
Drag out to their last dregs and I resume
On such legs as are left me, in such heart
As I can manage, remember to go home,
My taste will not have turned insensitive
To honey and bread old purity could love.

GWENDOLYN BROOKS

Tragedy. She considered that word. On the whole, she felt, life was more comedy than tragedy. Nearly everything that happened had its comic element, not too well buried, either. Sooner or later one could find something to laugh at in almost every situation. That was what, in the last analysis, could keep folks from going mad. The truth was, if you got a good Tragedy out of a lifetime, one good, ripping tragedy, thorough, unridiculous, bottom-scraping, not the issue of human stupidity, you were doing, she thought, very well, you were doing very well.

GWENDOLYN BROOKS, *Maud Martha*

THE NIAGARA RIVER

As though
the river were
a floor, we position
our table and chairs
upon it, eat, and
have conversation.
As it moves along,
we notice—as
calmly as though
dining room paintings
were being replaced—
the changing scenes
along the shore. We
do know, we do
know this is the
Niagara River, but
it is hard to remember
what that means.

KAY RYAN

INNOCENCE

They laughed at one I loved—
The triangular hill that hung
Under the Big Forth. They said
That I was bounded by the whitethorn hedges
Of the little farm and did not know the world.
But I knew that love's doorway to life
Is the same doorway everywhere.

Ashamed of what I loved
I flung her from me and called her a ditch
Although she was smiling at me with violets.

But now I am back in her briary arms
The dew of an Indian Summer morning lies
On bleached potato-stalks—
What age am I?

I do not know what age I am,
I am no mortal age;
I know nothing of women,
Nothing of cities,
I cannot die
Unless I walk outside these whitethorn hedges.

PATRICK KAVANAGH

In one of her notebooks a young French woman (Simone Weil) wrote, "One must believe in the reality of time. Otherwise one is just dreaming. For years I have recognized this flaw in myself, the importance it represents, and yet I have done nothing to get rid of it. What excuse could I be able to offer? Hasn't it increased in me since the age of ten?"

To resist the reality of time is to resist leaving childhood behind. She called this resistance a flaw in herself, but is it? The self is not the soul, and it is the soul (coherence) that lives for nine years on earth in a potential state of liberty and harmony. Its openness to metamorphosis is usually sealed up during these early years until the self replaces the soul as the fist of survival.

FANNY HOWE, *The Winter Sun*

SINGING IN MY DIFFICULT MOUNTAINS

Helot for what time there is
in the baptist hegemony of death.
For what time there is summer,
island, cornice. Weeping
and singing of what declines
into the earth. But of having,
not of not having. What abounds.
Amazed morning after morning
by the yielding. What times there are.
My fine house that love is.

JACK GILBERT

OLD FISHERMAN WITH GUITAR

A formal exercise for withered fingers.
  The head is bent,
    The eyes half closed, the tune
Lingers
    And beats, a gentle wing the west had thrown
  Against his breakwater wall with salt savage lament.

So fierce and sweet the song on the plucked string,
  Know now for truth
    Those hands have cut from the net
The strong
    Crab-eaten corpse of Jock washed from a boat
  One old winter, and gathered the mouth of Thora to his mouth.

GEORGE MACKAY BROWN

Heimat is one of those German words that is almost beyond trans-
lation. A dictionary [. . .] will typically give you a simple answer:
home, place of origin or subsequent association. In truth, it is so
much more. Drawing deeply on landscape and culture, music, and
smell, the word, along with all its associations, evokes an almost
visceral response, sparking feelings of longing and security, loss and
melancholia. It goes to the gut. It is, in that charged term of our
times, ultimately about identity.

FREDERICK STUDEMANN, "HOMEWARD BOUND"

"While I was downstairs before, on my way here, listening to that
woman sing, it struck me all of a sudden how much suffering she
must have had to go through—to sing like that. It's *repulsive* to
think you have to suffer that much."

JAMES BALDWIN, "SONNY'S BLUES"

LOCALS

They peopled landscapes casually like trees,
being there richly, never having gone there,
and whether clanning in cities or village-thin stands
were reticent as trees with those not born there,
and their fate, like trees, was seldom in their hands.

Others to them were always one of two
evils: the colonist or refugee.
They stared back, half-disdaining us, half-fearing;
inferring from our looks their destiny
as preservation or as clearing.

I envied them. To be local was to know
which team to support: the local team;
where to drop in for a pint with mates: the local;
best of all to feel by birthright welcome
anywhere; be everywhere a local . . .

Bedouin-Brython-Algonquins; always there
before you; the original prior claim
that made your being anywhere intrusive.
There, doubtless, in Eden before Adam
wiped them out and settled in with Eve.

Whether at home or away, whether kids
playing or saying what they wanted,
or adults chatting, waiting for a bus,
or, in their well-tended graves, the contented dead,
there were always locals, and they were never us.

JAMES LASDUN

It is not true that it doesn't matter where you live, that you are in Hartford or Dallas merely yourself. Also it is not true that all are linked naturally to their regions. Many are flung down carelessly at birth and they experience the diminishment and sometimes the pleasant truculence of their random misplacement. Americans who are Germans, Germans who are Frenchmen, like Heine perhaps.

The stain of place hangs on not as a birthright but as a sort of artifice, a bit of cosmetic. I place myself among the imports, those jarring and jarred pieces that sit in the closet among the matching china sets. I have no relations that I know of born outside the South and hardly any living outside it even today. Nevertheless, I am afraid of the country night and its honest slumbers, uneasy even in the daylight with "original settlers" and old American stock. The highway, the asphalt paths, the thieves, the contaminated skies like a suffocating cloak of mangy fur, the millions in their boroughs—that is truly home.

ELIZABETH HARDWICK, Sleepless Nights

THIS

isn't "making" love,
This is feeding off the substance of
what was made when we were made.

This is the body unafraid
of the soul. This is Abelardian glut
in a starved school.

This is negation of adulthood's rule
that talks by rote.
This is travelling out to where

a curved adventure
splashes on planes of sunlight to become
one perfectly remembered room:

white walls, white wings of curtain, window
screened but open
wide to cricket chirr in a field where no

discovery is new.
This is the always has been. What we do
is home. And this is I and you.

ANNE STEVENSON

EARTHMOVING MALEDICTION

Bulldoze the bed where we made love,
bulldoze the goddamn room.
Let rubble be our evidence
and wreck our home.

I can't give touching up by inches,
can't give beating up
by heart. So set
the comforter on fire, and turn the dirt

to some advantage—palaces of
pigweed, treasuries of turd. The fist
will vindicate the hand; the tooth
and nail refuse to burn, and I

must not look back, as
Mrs. Lot was named for such
a little—something
in a cemetery,

or a man. Bulldoze the coupled
ploys away, the cute exclusives
in the social mall. We dwell

on earth, where beds are brown,
where swoops are fell. Bulldoze
it all, up to the pearly gates:

if paradise comes down
there is no other hell.

HEATHER MCHUGH

INDIAN BOARDING SCHOOL: THE RUNAWAYS

Home's the place we head for in our sleep.
Boxcars stumbling north in dreams
don't wait for us. We catch them on the run.
The rails, old lacerations that we love,
shoot parallel across the face and break
just under Turtle Mountains. Riding scars
you can't get lost. Home is the place they cross.

The lame guard strikes a match and makes the dark
less tolerant. We watch through cracks in boards
as the land starts rolling, rolling till it hurts
to be here, cold in regulation clothes.
We know the sheriff's waiting at midrun
to take us back. His car is dumb and warm.
The highway doesn't rock, it only hums
like a wing of long insults. The worn-down welts
of ancient punishments lead back and forth.

All runaways wear dresses, long green ones,
the color you would think shame was. We scrub
the sidewalks down because it's shameful work.
Our brushes cut the stone in watered arcs
and in the soak frail outlines shiver clear
a moment, things us kids pressed on the dark
face before it hardened, pale, remembering
delicate old injuries, the spines of names and leaves.

LOUISE ERDRICH

Our songs travel the earth. We sing to one another. Not a single note is ever lost and no song is original. They all come from the same place and go back to a time when only the stones howled.

LOUISE ERDRICH, The Master Butchers Singing Club

THE IDEA OF ANCESTRY

1

Taped to the wall of my cell are 47 pictures: 47 black
faces: my father, mother, grandmothers (1 dead), grand-
fathers (both dead), brothers, sisters, uncles, aunts,
cousins (1st & 2nd), nieces, and nephews. They stare
across the space at me sprawling on my bunk. I know
their dark eyes, they know mine. I know their style,
they know mine. I am all of them, they are all of me;
they are farmers, I am a thief, I am me, they are thee.

I have at one time or another been in love with my mother,
1 grandmother, 2 sisters, 2 aunts (1 went to the asylum),
and 5 cousins. I am now in love with a 7-yr-old niece
(she sends me letters written in large block print, and
her picture is the only one that smiles at me).

I have the same name as 1 grandfather, 3 cousins, 3 nephews,
and 1 uncle. The uncle disappeared when he was 15, just took
off and caught a freight (they say). He's discussed each year
when the family has a reunion, he causes uneasiness in
the clan, he is an empty space. My father's mother, who is 93
and who keeps the Family Bible with everybody's birth dates
(and death dates) in it, always mentions him. There is no
place in her Bible for "whereabouts unknown."

2

Each fall the graves of my grandfathers call me, the brown
hills and red gullies of mississippi send out their electric
messages, galvanizing my genes. Last yr/like a salmon quitting

the cold ocean-leaping and bucking up his birth stream/I
hitchhiked my way from LA with 16 caps in my pocket and a
monkey on my back. And I almost kicked it with the kinfolks.
I walked barefooted in my grandmother's backyard/I smelled the old
land and the woods/I sipped cornwhiskey from fruit jars with the
   men/
I flirted with the women/I had a ball till the caps ran out
and my habit came down. That night I looked at my grandmother
and split/my guts were screaming for junk/but I was almost
contented/I had almost caught up with me.
(The next day in Memphis I cracked a croaker's crib for a fix.)

This yr there is a gray stone wall damming my stream, and when
the falling leaves stir my genes, I pace my cell or flop on my bunk
and stare at 47 black faces across the space. I am all of them,
they are all of me, I am me, they are thee, and I have no children
to float in the space between.

ETHERIDGE KNIGHT

BIRTHPLACE: NEW ROCHELLE

Returning to that house
And the rounded rocks of childhood—They have lasted well.

A world of things.

An aging man,
The knuckles of my hand
So jointed! I am this?

                    The house
My father's once, and the ground. There is a color of his times
In the sun's light

A generation's mark.
It intervenes. My child,
Not now a child, our child
Not altogether lone in a lone universe that suffers time
Like stones in sun. For we do not.

                                        GEORGE OPPEN

For every single person needs to be reconciled to a world into which he was born a stranger and to which, to the extent of his distinct uniqueness, he always remains a stranger.

HANNAH ARENDT, "UNDERSTANDING AND POLITICS"

Though white is
the color of worship and of mourning, he

is not here to worship and he is too wise
to mourn—a life prisoner but reconciled.

MARIANNE MOORE, "ELEPHANTS"

ö

Shape the lips to an *o*, say *a*.
That's *island*.

One word of Swedish has changed the whole neighborhood.
When I look up, the yellow house on the corner
is a galleon stranded in flowers. Around it

the wind. Even the high roar of a leaf-mulcher
could be the horn-blast from a ship
as it skirts to the misted shoals.

We don't need much more to keep things going.
Families complete themselves
and refuse to budge from the present,
the present extends its glass forehead to sea
(backyard breezes, scattered cardinals)

and if, one evening, the house on the corner
took off over the marshland,
neither I nor my neighbour
would be amazed. Sometimes

a word is found so right it trembles
at the slightest explanation.
You start out with one thing, end
up with another, and nothing's
like it used to be, not even the future.

RITA DOVE

The hard part
Is to find yourself at home with where and what you are
And still remain amazed.

JOHN KOETHE, "BEYOND BELIEF"

A HOLE IN THE FLOOR

for René Magritte

The carpenter's made a hole
In the parlor floor, and I'm standing
Staring down into it now
At four o'clock in the evening,
As Schliemann stood when his shovel
Knocked on the crowns of Troy.

A clean-cut sawdust sparkles
On the grey, shaggy laths,
And here is a cluster of shavings
From the time when the floor was laid.
They are silvery-gold, the color
Of Hesperian apple-parings.

Kneeling, I look in under
Where the joists go into hiding.
A pure street, faintly littered
With bits and strokes of light,
Enters the long darkness
Where its parallels will meet.

The radiator-pipe
Rises in middle distance
Like a shuttered kiosk, standing
Where the only news is night.
Here it's not painted green,
As it is in the visible world.

For God's sake, what am I after?
Some treasure, or tiny garden?
Or that untrodden place,
The house's very soul,
Where time has stored our footbeats
And the long skein of our voices?

Not these, but the buried strangeness
Which nourishes the known:
That spring from which the floor-lamp
Drinks now a wilder bloom,
Inflaming the damask love-seat
And the whole dangerous room.

RICHARD WILBUR

OLD HOUSES

Aunt Martha bustles
From room to room
Between attic and basement,
With duster and broom.

Like an oven grenade,
In cobwebby corners
Her broom explodes
A babel of wonders.

Her summer crusade
Havocs the bugs.
Like an enfilade,
She rakes the rugs.

The sound and fury
Of table and bed
Whirs a panic of sparrows
To the oaks overhead.

Untenable grows
The vast of the house
For even the ghost
Of Lazarus' mouse.

The fogies convert
Back fences to staffs
And sow their gossip
With Pharisee laughs:

Aunt Martha's scowl
Is a lithograph's.

As the fogies watch
Her attic lairs
Jettison the junk
Of heirloom wares,
She shouts: "Old houses
Need cleaning upstairs!"

MELVIN B. TOLSON

TOWARD THE SOLSTICE

The thirtieth of November.
Snow is starting to fall.
A peculiar silence is spreading
over the fields, the maple grove.
It is the thirtieth of May,
rain pours on ancient bushes, runs
down the youngest blade of grass.
I am trying to hold in one steady glance
all the parts of my life.
A spring torrent races
on this old slanting roof,
the slanted field below
thickens with winter's first whiteness.
Thistles dried to sticks in last year's wind
stand nakedly in the green,
stand sullenly in the slowly whitening,
field.

My brain glows
more violently, more avidly
the quieter, the thicker
the quilt of crystals settles,
the louder, more relentlessly
the torrent beats itself out
on the old boards and shingles.
It is the thirtieth of May,
the thirtieth of November,
a beginning or an end,
we are moving into the solstice
and there is so much here

I still do not understand.
If I could make sense of how
my life is still tangled
with dead weeds, thistles,
enormous burdocks, burdens
slowly shifting under
this first fall of snow,
beaten by this early, racking rain
calling all new life to declare itself strong
or die,
      if I could know
in what language to address
the spirits that claim a place
beneath these low and simple ceilings,
tenants that neither speak nor stir
yet dwell in mute insistence
till I can feel utterly ghosted in this house.

If history is a spider-thread
spun over and over though brushed away
it seems I might some twilight
or dawn in the hushed country light
discern its greyness stretching
from molding or doorframe, out
into the empty dooryard
and following it climb
the path into the pinewoods,
tracing from tree to tree
in the failing light, in the slowly
lucidifying day

its constant, purposive trail,
till I reach whatever cellar hole
filling with snowflakes or lichen,
whatever fallen shack
or unremembered clearing
I am meant to have found
and there, under the first or last
star, trusting to instinct
the words would come to mind
I have failed or forgotten to say
year after year, winter
after summer, the right rune
to ease the hold of the past
upon the rest of my life
and ease my hold on the past.

If some rite of separation
is still unaccomplished
between myself and the long-gone
tenants of this house,
between myself and my childhood,
and the childhood of my children,
it is I who have neglected
to perform the needed acts,
set water in corners, light and eucalyptus
in front of mirrors,
or merely pause and listen
to my own pulse vibrating
lightly as falling snow,
relentlessly as the rainstorm,

and hear what it has been saying.
It seems I am still waiting
for them to make some clear demand
some articulate sound or gesture,
for release to come from anywhere
but from inside myself.

A decade of cutting away
dead flesh, cauterizing
old scars ripped open over and over
and still it is not enough.
A decade of performing
the loving humdrum acts
of attention to this house
transplanting lilac suckers,
washing panes, scrubbing
wood-smoke from splitting paint,
sweeping stairs, brushing the thread
of the spider aside,
and so much yet undone,
a woman's work, the solstice nearing,
and my hand still suspended
as if above a letter
I long and dread to close.

ADRIENNE RICH

Space has a spiritual equivalent and can heal what is divided and burdensome in us. My grandchildren will probably use space shuttles for a honeymoon trip or to recover from heart attacks, but closer to home we might also learn how to carry space inside ourselves in the effortless way we carry our skins. Space represents sanity, not a life purified, dull, or "spaced out" but one that might accommodate intelligently any idea or situation.

From the clayey soil of northern Wyoming is mined bentonite, which is used as a filler in candy, gum, and lipstick. We Americans are great in-fillers, as if what we have, what we are, is not enough. We have a cultural tendency toward denial, but, being affluent we strangle ourselves with what we can buy. We have only to look at the houses we build to see how we build *against* space, the way we drink against pain and loneliness. We fill up space as if it were a pie shell, with things whose opacity further obstructs our ability to see what is already there.

GRETEL EHRLICH, *The Solace of Open Spaces*

In experience, the meaning of space often merges with that of place. "Space" is more abstract than "place." What begins as undifferentiated space becomes place as we get to know it better and endow it with value. Architects talk about the spatial qualities of place; they can equally well speak of the locational (place) qualities of space. The ideas "space" and "place" require each other for definition. From the security and stability of place we are aware of the openness, freedom, and threat of space, and vice versa. Furthermore, if we think of space as that which allows movement, then place is pause; each pause in movement makes it possible for location to be transformed into place.

YI-FU TUAN, *Space and Place: The Perspective of Experience*

MOVING IN

*"It is the worst of luck to bring
into a new house from the old
bread salt or broomstick."*

Salt Bread and Broom
be still.
I leave you guardian
against gone places
I have loved
your loss
in a green promise
making new
Salt
Bread
and Broom
remove me from the was
I still am
to now
becoming
here this house
forever blessed.

AUDRE LORDE

There's nothing that makes you so aware of the improvisation of human existence as a song unfinished. Or an old address book.

CARSON MCCULLERS, "THE SOJOURNER"

HOUSECOOLING

Those ashes shimmering dully in the fireplace,
like tarnished fish scales? I swept them out.
Those tiny tumbleweeds of dust that stalled
against a penny or a paperclip under the bed?
I lay along the grain of the floorboards
and stared each pill into the vacuum's mouth.
I loved that house and I was moving out.

What do you want to do when you grow up?
they asked, and I never said, *I want to haunt*
a house. But I grew pale. The way the cops "lift"
fingerprints, that's how I touched the house.
The way one of my sons would stand in front
of me and say, *I'm outta here,* and he would mean
it, his crisp, heart-creasing husk delivering

a kind of telegram from wherever the rest of him
had gone—that's how I laved and scoured
and patrolled the house, and how I made my small
withdrawals and made my wan way outta there.
And then I was gone. I took what I could.
Each smudge I left, each slur, each whorl, I left
for love, but love of what I cannot say.

WILLIAM MATTHEWS

WHAT GOOD POEMS ARE FOR

To sit on a shelf in the cabin across the lake
where the young man and the young woman
have come to live—there are only a few books
in this dwelling, and one of them
is this book of poems.

                To be like plants
on a sunlit windowsill
of a city apartment—all the hours of care
that go into them, the tending and watering,
and yet to the casual eye they are just present
—a brief moment of enjoyment.
Only those who work on the plant
know how slowly it grows
and changes, almost dies from its own causes
or neglect, or how other plants
can be started from this one
and used elsewhere in the house
or given to friends.
But everyone notices the absence of plants
in a residence
even those who don't have plants themselves.

There is also (though this is more rare)
Bob Smith's story about the man in the bar up north,
a man in his 50s, taking a poem from a new book Bob showed him
around from table to table, reading it aloud
to each group of drinkers because, he kept saying,
the poem was about work he did, what he knew about,
written by somebody like himself.

But where could he take it
except from table to table, past the *Fuck offs*
and the *Hey, that's pretty goods?* Over the noise
of the jukebox and the bar's TV,
past the silence of the lake,
a person is speaking
in a world full of people talking.
Out of all that is said, these particular words
put down roots in someone's mind
so that he or she likes to have them here—
these words no one was paid to write
that live with us for a while
in a small container
on the ledge where the light enters

TOM WAYMAN

A POSTCARD FROM THE VOLCANO

Children picking up our bones
Will never know that these were once
As quick as foxes on the hill;

And that in autumn, when the grapes
Made sharp air sharper by their smell
These had a being, breathing frost;

And least will guess that with our bones
We left much more, left what still is
The look of things, left what we felt

At what we saw. The spring clouds blow
Above the shuttered mansion-house,
Beyond our gate and the windy sky

Cries out a literate despair.
We knew for long the mansion's look
And what we said of it became

A part of what it is . . . Children,
Still weaving budded aureoles,
Will speak our speech and never know,

Will say of the mansion that it seems
As if he that lived there left behind
A spirit storming in blank walls,

A dirty house in a gutted world,
A tatter of shadows peaked to white,
Smeared with the gold of the opulent sun.

WALLACE STEVENS

I thought on the train how utterly we have forsaken the Earth, in the sense of excluding it from our thoughts. There are but few who consider its physical hugeness, its rough enormity. It is still a disparate monstrosity, full of solitudes & barrens & wilds. It still dwarfs & terrifies & crushes. The rivers still roar, the mountains still crash, the winds still shatter. Man is an affair of cities. His gardens & orchards & fields are mere scrapings. Somehow, however, he has managed to shut out the face of the giant from his windows. But the giant is there, nevertheless.

WALLACE STEVENS, *Souvenirs and Prophecies*

STUDY THE MASTERS

like my aunt timmie.
it was her iron,
or one like hers,
that smoothed the sheets
the master poet slept on.
home or hotel, what matters is
he lay himself down on her handiwork
and dreamed. she dreamed too, words:
some cherokee, some masai and some
huge and particular as hope.
if you had heard her
chanting as she ironed
you would understand form and line
and discipline and order and
america.

LUCILLE CLIFTON

Nor is there singing school but studying
Monuments of its own magnificence.

WILLIAM BUTLER YEATS, "SAILING TO BYZANTIUM"

It is not so much what you sang, as that you kept alive, in so many
of our ancestors, *the notion of song.*

ALICE WALKER, *In Search of Our Mothers' Gardens*

BALANCE

He watch her like a coonhound watch a tree.
What might explain the metamorphosis
he underwent when she paraded by
with tea-cakes, in her fresh and shabby dress?
(As one would carry water from a well—
straight-backed, high-headed, like a diadem,
with careful grace so that no drop will spill—
she balanced, almost brimming, her one name.)

She think she something, stuck-up island bitch.
Chopping wood, hanging laundry on the line,
and tantalizingly within his reach,
she honed his body's yearning to a keen,
sharp point. And on that point she balanced life.
That hoe Diverne think she Marse Tyler's wife.

MARILYN NELSON

43

THIS ROOM AND EVERYTHING IN IT

Lie still now
while I prepare for my future,
certain hard days ahead,
when I'll need what I know so clearly this moment.

I am making use
of the one thing I learned
of all the things my father tried to teach me:
the art of memory.

I am letting this room
and everything in it
stand for my ideas about love
and its difficulties.

I'll let your love-cries,
those spacious notes
of a moment ago,
stand for distance.

Your scent,
that scent
of spice and a wound,
I'll let stand for mystery.

Your sunken belly
is the daily cup
of milk I drank
as a boy before morning prayer.
The sun on the face

of the wall
is God, the face
I can't see, my soul,

and so on, each thing
standing for a separate idea,
and those ideas forming the constellation
of my greater idea.
And one day, when I need
to tell myself something intelligent
about love,

I'll close my eyes
and recall this room and everything in it:
My body is estrangement.
This desire, perfection.
Your closed eyes my extinction.
Now I've forgotten my
idea. The book
on the windowsill, riffled by wind . . .
the even-numbered pages are
the past, the odd-
numbered pages, the future.
The sun is
God, your body is milk . . .

useless, useless . . .
your cries are song, my body's not me . . .
no good . . . my idea
has evaporated . . . your hair is time, your thighs are song . . .

it had something to do
with death . . . it had something
to do with love.

LI-YOUNG LEE

from SABBATH POEMS, 1997

I

Best of any song
is bird song
in the quiet, but first
you must have the quiet.

II

Even while I dreamed I prayed that what I saw was only fear and no
    foretelling,
for I saw the last known landscape destroyed for the sake
of the objective, the soil bulldozed, the rock blasted.
Those who had wanted to go home would never get there now.

I visited the offices where for the sake of the objective the planners
    planned
at blank desks set in rows. I visited the loud factories
where the machines were made that would drive ever forward
toward the objective. I saw the forest reduced to stumps and gullies;
    I saw
the poisoned river, the mountain cast into the valley;
I came to the city that nobody recognized because it looked like
    every other city.
I saw the passages worn by the unnumbered
footfalls of those whose eyes were fixed upon the objective.

Their passage had obliterated the graves and the monuments
of those who had died in pursuit of the objective
and who had long ago forever been forgotten, according
to the invariable rule that those who have forgotten forget

that they have forgotten. Men and women and children now
    pursued the objective
as if nobody ever had pursued it before.

The races and the sexes now intermingled perfectly in pursuit of
    the objective.
The once-enslaved, the once-oppressed were now free
to sell themselves to the highest bidder
and to enter the best-paying prisons
in pursuit of the objective, which was the destruction of all enemies,
which was the destruction of all obstacles, which was to clear the way
to victory which was to clear the way to promotion, to salvation,
    to progress,
to the completed sale, to the signature
on the contract, which was to clear the way
to self-realization, to self-creation, from which nobody who ever
    wanted to go home
would ever get there now, for every remembered place
had been displaced; the signposts had been bent to the ground and
    covered over.

Every place had been displaced, every love
unloved, every vow unsworn, every word unmeant
to make way for the passage of the crowd
of the individuated, the autonomous, the self-actuated, the homeless
with their many eyes opened only toward the objective
which they did not yet perceive in the far distance,
having never known where they were going,
having never known where they came from.

III

I was wakened from my dream of the ruined world by the sound
of rain falling slowly onto the dry earth of my place in time.
On the parched garden, the cracked-open pastures,
the dusty grape leaves, the brittled grass, the drooping foliage of the
    woods,
fell still the quiet rain.

IV

"You see," my mother said, and laughed,
knowing I knew the passage
she was remembering, "finally you lose
everything." She had lost
parents, husband, friends, youth,
health, most comforts, many hopes.

Deaf, asleep in her chair, awakened
by a hand's touch, she would look up
and smile in welcome as quiet
as if she had seen us coming.

She watched, curious and affectionate,
the sparrows, titmice, and chickadees
she fed at her kitchen window—
where did they come from, where
did they go? No matter.
They came and went as freely as
in the time of her old age
her children came and went,
uncaptured, but fed.

And I, walking in the first spring
of her absence, know again
her inextinguishable delight:
the wild bluebells, the yellow
celandine, violets purple
and white, twinleaf, bloodroot,
larkspur, the rue anemone
light, light under the big trees,
and overhead the redbud blooming,
the redbird singing,
the oak leaves like flowers still
unfolding, and the blue sky.

V

The lovers know the loveliness
That is not of their bodies only
(Though they be lovely) but is of
Their bodies given up to love.

They find the open-heartedness
Of two desires which both are lonely
Until by dying they have their living,
And gain all they have lost in giving,

Each offering the desired desire.
Beyond what time requires, they are
What they surpass themselves to make;
They give the pleasure that they take.

VI

Now, as a man learning
the limits of time, I look anew
at a familiar carving: a ring
of granite drawing to a circle

all space around it, and enclosing
a circle. In cross section, the stone
itself is square. It doubles
the superficial strip of Möbius

and thus makes of two surfaces
a solid, dimensioned
as the body, a pure thought
shaped in stone. One surface

is rough, the other smooth,
to invite hand or eye into
its windings, to remind the mind
in its travels, the long and far

of its restless reckoning,
that where it comes from
and where it is going
are nowhere in the distance,

not in the future or the past,
but are forever here
now. The stone turns
without limit within itself,

dark within light, light
within dark. What is above
descends, what is below rises.
So the carver wrought it out

until it came to rest.
So what is inward turns outward
as does, we are told, the Kingdom of God.
So we contain that which contains us.

So the departed come to light.

VII

There is a day
when the road neither
comes nor goes, and the way
is not a way but a place.

WENDELL BERRY

In this awakening there has been a good deal of pain. When I lived in other places I looked on their evils with the curious eye of a traveler; I was not responsible for them; it cost me nothing to be a critic, for I had not been there long, and I did not feel that I would stay. But here, now that I am both native and citizen, there is no immunity to what is wrong. It is impossible to escape the sense that I am involved in history. What I am has been to a considerable extent determined by what my forefathers were, by how they chose to treat this place while they lived in it; the lives of most of them diminished it, and limited its possibilities, and narrowed its future. And every day I am confronted by the question of what inheritance I will leave. What do I have that I am using up? For it has been our history that each generation in this place has been less welcome to it than the last. There has been less here for them. At each arrival there has been less fertility in the soil, and a larger inheritance of destructive precedent and shameful history.

I am forever being crept up on and newly startled by the realization that my people established themselves here by killing or driving out the original possessors, by the awareness that people were once bought and sold here by my people, by the sense of the violence they have done to their own kind and to each other and to the earth, by the evidence of their persistent failure to serve either the place or their own community in it. I am forced, against all my hopes and inclinations, to regard the history of my people here as the progress of the doom of what I value most in the world: the life and health of the earth, the peacefulness of human communities and households.

And so here, in the place I love more than any other and where I have chosen among all other places to live my life, I am more painfully divided within myself than I could be in any other place.

WENDELL BERRY, *The Long-Legged House*

Home is a notion that only nations of the homeless fully appreciate and only the uprooted comprehend.

WALLACE STEGNER, Angle of Repose

This unhoused, exiled Satan was perhaps the heavenly patron of all exiles, all unhoused people, all those who were torn from their place and left floating, half-this, half-that, denied the rooted person's comforting, defining sense of having solid ground beneath their feet.

SALMAN RUSHDIE, Joseph Anton: A Memoir

SHEMA

You who live secure
In your warm houses,
Who return at evening to find
Hot food and friendly faces:

    Consider whether this is a man,
    Who labours in the mud
    Who knows no peace
    Who fights for a crust of bread
    Who dies at a yes or a no.
    Consider whether this is a woman,
    Without hair or name
    With no more strength to remember
    Eyes empty and womb cold
    As a frog in winter.

Consider that this has been:
I commend these words to you.
Engrave them on your hearts
When you are in your house, when you walk on your way,
When you go to bed, when you rise.
Repeat them to your children.
Or may your house crumble,
Disease render you powerless,
Your offspring avert their faces from you.

PRIMO LEVI
(TRANSLATED FROM THE ITALIAN
BY RUTH FELDMAN AND BRIAN SWANN)

THE GUEST ELLEN AT THE SUPPER FOR STREET PEOPLE

The unclean spirits cry out in the body
Or mind of the guest Ellen in a loud voice
Torment me not, and in the fury of her unclean
Hands beating the air in some kind of unending torment—
Nobody witnessing could possibly know the event
That cast upon her the spell of this enchantment.

Almost all the guests are under some kind of enchantment:
Of being poor day after day in the same body;
Of being witness still to some obscene event;
Of listening all the time to somebody's voice
Whispering in the ear things divine or unclean,
In the quotidian of unending torment.

One has to keep thinking there was some source of torment,
Something that happened someplace else, unclean.
One has to keep talking in a reasonable voice
About things done, say, by a father's body
To or upon the body of Ellen, in enchantment
Helpless, still by the unforgotten event

Enchanted, still in the old forgotten event
A prisoner of love, filthy Ellen in her torment,
Guest Ellen in the dining hall in her body,
Hands beating the air in her enchantment,
Sitting alone, gabbling in her garbled voice
The narrative of the spirits of the unclean.

She is wholly the possessed one of the unclean.
Maybe the spirits came from the river. The enchantment

Entered her, maybe, in the Northeast Kingdom. The torment,
A thing of the waters, gratuitous event,
Came up out of the waters and entered her body
And lived in her in torment and cried out in her voice.

It speaks itself over and over again in her voice,
Cursing maybe or not a familiar obscene event
Or only the pure event of original enchantment
From the birth of the river waters, the pure unclean
Rising from the source of things, in a figure of torment
Seeking out Ellen, finding its home in her poor body.

Her body witness is, so also is her voice,
Of torment coming from unknown event;
Unclean is the nature and name of the enchantment.

DAVID FERRY

58

THE MASTER'S HOUSE

To wave from the porch
To let go of the grudge
To disrobe
To recall Ethel Rosenberg's green polka-dotted dress
To call your father and say *I'd forgotten how nice everyone in these
    red states can be*
To hear him say *Yes, long as you don't move in next door*
To recall every drawn curtain in the apartments you have lived
To find yourself at 33 at a vast expanse with nary a papyrus of
    guidance, with nary a voice, a muse, a model
To finally admit out loud then *I want to go home*
To have a dinner party of intellectuals with a bell, long-armed,
    lightly-tongued, at each setting
To sport your dun gown
To revel in face serums
To be a well-calibrated burn victim to fight the signs of aging
To assure financial health
To be lavender sachets and cedar lining and all the ways the rich
    might hide their rot
To eye the master's bone china
To pour diuretic in his coffee and think this erosive to the state
To disrobe when the agent asks you to
To find a spot on any wall to stare into
To develop the ability to leave an entire nation thusly, just by staring
    at a spot on the wall, as the lead-vested agent names article by
    article what to remove
To do this in order to do the other thing, the wild thing
To say this is my filmdom, The Master's House, and I gaze upon it
    and it is good
To discuss desalinization plants and de terroir

To date briefly a banker, a lapsed Marxist, and hear him on the
  phone speaking in billions of dollars, its residue over the clear
  bulbs of his eyes, as he turns to look upon your nudity
To fantasize publishing a poem in the *New Yorker* eviscerating his
  little need
To set a bell at each intellectual's table setting ringing idea after idea,
  and be the simple-footed help, rushing to say *Yes?*
To disrobe when the agent asks you to
To find a spot on any wall to stare into
To develop the ability to leave an entire nation thusly, just by staring
  at a spot on the wall
To say this is my filmdom, The Master's House
To recall the Settler who from behind his mobile phone said *I'm
  filming you for God*
To recall this sad God, God of the mobile phone camera, God of the
  small black globe and pixelated eye above the blackjack table at
  Harrah's and the metal, toothed pit of Qalandia checkpoint the
  same
To recall the Texan that held the shotgun to your father's chest,
  sending him falling backward, pleading, and the words came to
  him in Farsi
To be jealous of this, his most desperate language
To lament the fact of your lamentations in English, English being
  your first defeat
To finally admit out loud then *I want to go home*
To stand outside your grandmother's house
To know, for example, that in Farsi the present perfect is called the
  relational past, and is used at times to describe a historic event
  whose effect is still relevant today, transcending the past

To say, for example, *Shah dictator bude-ast* translates to *The Shah was a dictator,* but more literally to *The Shah* is *was a dictator*

To have a tense of is-was, the residue of it over the clear bulb of your eyes

To walk cemetery after cemetery in these States and nary a gravestone reading *Solmaz*

To know no nation will be home until one does

To do this in order to do the other thing, the wild thing, though you've forgotten what it was

SOLMAZ SHARIF

FROM THE GARDEN OF THE WOMEN ONCE FALLEN

Thyme

Woman alone, living
in a tenement of enmity.
One room of back-biting
standpipe flowing strife.

Recall one dry Sunday
of rice and peas and no meat
how you boiled a handful
of fresh green thyme

to carry the smell of Sunday
as usual.
Thyme, herb of contraction
rising as steaming incense
of save-face.

When you dwell among enemies
you never make them salt your pot.
You never make them know
your want.

Of Bitterness Herbs

You knotted the spite blooms into a bouquet-garni
to flavor stock for sour soups and confusion stews.
Now no one will dine with you.

A diet of bitterness is self consuming.
Such herbs are best destroyed, rooted out
from the garden of the necessary, preordained past.

Bitter herbs grow luxuriant where the grudgeful crow
dropped its shadow, starting a compost heap of need in you
to spray malicious toxins over all flowers in our rose gardens.

Bitterness herbs bake bad-minded bread, are good for little
except pickling green-eyed gall stones, then eaten alone
from wooden spoons of must-suck-salt.

In the Time of Late-Blooming Pumpkins

In this garden, water walks
and water walking enters
belly of pumpkin.

This means you are growing
big from within, all ripeness,
though somebody (Jeremiah?)

shouts from outside the garden wall
"You are all conceived in sin"
but that is just some false prophet

negative and bad mouthing.
For in this new garden
of fresh start over

with its mysteries of walking water,
give thanks for late summer's
rose afternoons shading

into amethyst, then deepening
into red water grass evenings,
time of late-blooming pumpkins.

LORNA GOODISON

AT TIKAL

Mountains they knew, and jungle, the sun, the stars—
these seemed to be there. But even after they slashed
the jungle and burned it and planted the comforting corn,
they were discontent. They wanted the shape of things.
They imagined a world and it was as if it were there
—a world with stars in their places and rain that came
when they called. It closed them in. Stone by stone,
as they built this city, these temples, they built this world.
They believed it. This was the world, and they,
of course, were the people. Now trees make up
assemblies and crowd in the wide plazas. Trees
climb the stupendous steps and rubble them.
In the jungle, the temples are little mountains again.

It is always hard like this, not having a world,
to imagine one, to go to the far edge
apart and imagine, to wall whether in
or out, to build a kind of cage for the sake
of feeling the bars around us, to give shape to a world.
And oh, it is always a world and not the world.

WILLIAM BRONK

I loved the living essence of historical symbolism, in other words the instinct which has enabled us, like house martins, to build a world, an immense nest made of earth and sky, of life and death, and of two kinds of time, time present and time absent. I understood that it was saved from disintegration by the cohesive force contained in the transparently figurative quality of every particle of it.

BORIS PASTERNAK, *Second Birth*
(TRANSLATED FROM THE RUSSIAN BY
JON STALLWORTHY AND PETER FRANCE)

FABLE OF THE HOUSE

This is a house
and will be for a long time
itself because the air
has come to recognize it
and call it by name.
            "Hello, House,
the birds are getting ready
down in Bolivia to come back
and bother you again."
            With its eaves
the house is listening, "O brother,
o bother, the birds
again, and their seeds, their seeds
have trees and their trees have birds
and there we are again,
all over me and the morning
too loud for me and the men and women
running down my halls
crying for their children and their children
with birds on their knees.
O it is hard to be me, it is hard to house."

"Cheer up brother," says the air
"I care and care and hurry everywhere
at once, and wherever I go
are people and their things
and every thing must have its man
or woman, and every house
must have its birds. I endure the clouds
and their unseen attendants,

I endure the morning choked with light
and the evening drowned in darkness

and none of it bothers me. None of it
should bother you, after all
you are a nest of things
and what a thing is
is a kind of sleeping. Isn't that so?"

So so was it, that the house was fast asleep.

ROBERT KELLY

In the olden days, things were very different from what they are now. Everything had a soul, everything was more alive. When a caribou had been eaten, the meat grew again on the bones . . . The houses were alive, and could be moved with everything in them, and the people as well, from one place to another. They rose up with a rushing noise into the air and flew to the spot where the people wanted to go. In those days also, newly drifted snow would burn. There was life in all things. Snow shovels could go about by themselves, could move from one place to another without having to be carried. This is why we now, when in solitary places, never dare to stick a snow shovel into the snow. We are afraid lest it should come alive and go off on its own. So we always lay snow shovels down in the snow, so that they do not stand up. Thus all things were alive in the olden days.

AQIKHIVIK (AS TOLD TO KNUD RASMUSSEN),
Observations on the Intellectual Culture of the Caribou Eskimos

IF CHINA

If china, then only the kind
you wouldn't miss under the movers' shoes or the treads of a tank;
if a chair, then one that's not too comfortable, or
you'll regret getting up and leaving;
if clothes, then only what will fit in one suitcase;
if books, then those you know by heart;
if plans, then the ones you can give up
when it comes time for the next move,
to another street, another continent or epoch
or world:

who told you you could settle in?
who told you this or that would last forever?
didn't anyone tell you you'll never
in the world
feel at home here?

STANISŁAW BARAŃCZAK
(TRANSLATED FROM THE POLISH
BY MAGNUS J. KRYNSKI)

I always move in my heart between sad countries.

AGHA SHAHID ALI, "I DREAM I AM AT
THE GHAT OF THE ONLY WORLD"

One more truth about the condition we call exile is that it acceler-
ates tremendously one's otherwise professional flight—or drift—into
isolation, into an absolute perspective: into the condition in which
all one is left with is oneself and one's own language, with nobody
or nothing in between.

JOSEPH BRODSKY, "THE CONDITION WE CALL EXILE"

I think exile has given me many opportunities to face the heart of
darkness, which every human being must face ... This path leading to
the heart of darkness, some people may refuse to take it, some may
give up half-way through. It has given me the courage to go on.

BEI DAO, *Modern Chinese Literature,* VOL. 9

MAY 24, 1980

I have braved, for want of wild beasts, steel cages,
carved my term and nickname on bunks and rafters,
lived by the sea, flashed aces in an oasis,
dined with the-devil-knows-whom, in tails, on truffles.
From the height of a glacier I beheld half a world, the earthly
width. Twice have drowned, thrice let knives rake my nitty-gritty.
Quit the country that bore and nursed me.
Those who forgot me would make a city.
I have waded the steppes that saw yelling Huns in saddles,
worn the clothes nowadays back in fashion in every quarter,
planted rye, tarred the roofs of pigsties and stables,
guzzled everything save dry water.
I've admitted the sentries' third eye into my wet and foul
dreams. Munched the bread of exile; it's stale and warty.
Granted my lungs all sounds except the howl;
switched to a whisper. Now I am forty.
What should I say about my life? That it's long and abhors
    transparence.
Broken eggs make me grieve; the omelette, though, makes me vomit.
Yet until brown clay has been crammed down my larynx,
only gratitude will be gushing from it.

JOSEPH BRODSKY

EMPATHY

My love, I'm grateful tonight
Our listing bed isn't a raft
Precariously adrift
As we dodge the coast guard light,

And clasp hold of a girl and a boy.
I'm glad that we didn't wake
Our kids in the thin hours, to take
Not a thing, not a favorite toy,

And we didn't hand over our cash
To one of the smuggling rackets,
That we didn't buy cheap life jackets
No better than bright orange trash

And less buoyant. I'm glad that the dark
Above us is not deeply twinned
Beneath us, and moiled with wind,
And we don't scan the sky for a mark,

Any mark, that demarcates a shore
As the dinghy starts taking on water.
I'm glad that our six-year-old daughter,
Who can't swim, is a foot off the floor

In the bottom bunk, and our son
With his broken arm's high and dry,
That the ceiling is not seeping sky,
With our journey but hardly begun.

Empathy isn't generous,
It's selfish. It's not being nice
To say I would pay any price
Not to be those who'd die to be us.

A. E. STALLINGS

THE BOATMAN

We were thirty-one souls all, he said, on the gray-sick of sea
in a cold rubber boat, rising and falling in our filth.
By morning this didn't matter, no land was in sight,
all were soaked to the bone, living and dead.
We could still float, we said, from war to war.
What lay behind us but ruins of stone piled on ruins of stone?
City called "mother of the poor" surrounded by fields
of cotton and millet, city of jewelers and cloak-makers,
with the oldest church in Christendom and the Sword of Allah.
If anyone remains there now, he assures, they would be utterly alone.
There is a hotel named for it in Rome two hundred meters
from the Piazza di Spagna, where you can have breakfast under
the portraits of film stars. There the staff cannot do enough for you.
But I am talking nonsense again, as I have since that night
we fetched a child, not ours, from the sea, drifting face-
down in a life vest, its eyes taken by fish or the birds above us.
After that, Aleppo went up in smoke, and Raqqa came under a rain
of leaflets warning everyone to go. Leave, yes, but go where?
We lived through the Americans and Russians, through Americans
again, many nights of death from the clouds, mornings surprised
to be waking from the sleep of death, still unburied and alive
with no safe place. Leave, yes, we'll obey the leaflets, but go where?
To the sea to be eaten, to the shores of Europe to be caged?
To *camp misery* and *camp remain here*. I ask you then, where?
You tell me you are a poet. If so, our destination is the same.
I find myself now the boatman, driving a taxi at the end of the world.
I will see that you arrive safely, my friend, I will get you there.

CAROLYN FORCHÉ

"My mother tongue is foreign. Hence I am on easy terms with my strangeness," he said.

And added: "I have patiently forged my language out of words that were foreigners, making them into brothers."

And had he not written earlier: "I did not take your soul: I gave it to you"?

What is a foreigner?—One who makes you think you are at home.

EDMOND JABÈS, "NOTEBOOK, II"

VOCATIVE

English is my native
anguish. I was born here,
read here, teased and torn here.
Vocative, ablative,

locative, alive:
English was a dislocation
navigating oceans.
Wherever it arrived,

it broke and brokered words,
its little bits of Britain
pilfered, bartered, written,
looted, hoarded, heard.

Papa swapped a world
for shiny colored beads,
for dandelion seeds.
We are subject verbs.

The root word of my name
hooks a foreign land,
long-since-shifted sand
books cannot reclaim.

Graft of tongue, gift of dust,
mother and stranger, sing
the kedgeree, the everything
at once you've made of us.

AMIT MAJMUDAR

BILINGUAL/BILINGÜE

My father liked them separate, one there,
one here (allá y aquí), as if aware

that words might cut in two his daughter's heart
(el corazón) and lock the alien part

to what he was—his memory, his name
(su nombre)—with a key he could not claim.

"English outside this door, Spanish inside,"
he said, "y basta." But who can divide

the world, the word (mundo y palabra) from
any child? I knew how to be dumb

and stubborn (testaruda); late, in bed,
I hoarded secret syllables I read

until my tongue (mi lengua) learned to run
where his stumbled. And still the heart was one.

I like to think he knew that, even when,
proud (orgulloso) of his daughter's pen,

he stood outside mis versos, half in fear
of words he loved but wanted not to hear.

RHINA ESPAILLAT

FLINT-CHANT

Once upon a time a ditchpipe got left behind behind Azalea Industrial, back in the woods backing on to the Ashley, where old pitch-pines and loblollies grow wild. A mild pesticide-mist was falling and mingling with paper-mill smell and creosote oil the morning he found it. The boy shook and sheltered in its mouth awhile—*hoo-hoo! hey-O!*—and bent and went on in. It was like a cave but clean. He C-curved his spine against one wall to fit, and humming something, sucked his shirttail. He tuned his eyes to what low light there was and knuckle-drummed a line along his legs.

What the boy called inside-*oku* called him back. He was hooked right quick on the well-bottom peace of the pumicey concrete and how sounds sounded in there, and re-sounded. Tight-curled as he had to get—like a cling-shrimp one day, a pill-bug, a bass-clef, a bison's eye; an abalone (*ocean-ear!*), antler-arc, Ark-ant, apostrophe another— sure as clocks a cool clear under-creek would rise, and rinse him through, and runnel free. Hanging in a green-pine O outside were sun-heat and smaze and BB-fire and Mosquito Abatement. Inside there were water-limber words (and a picture-noisy nave), shades of shade.

ATSURO RILEY

Reverence toward the world can come with the belief that it is God-bearing. The wheatgrass stem bears the charge of the sacred. Here is sufficient impetus for a careful, courteous attentiveness to things that might be expected to end in an awful silence, the eye and feeling swallowed by root system, leaf shape, feather colour. But often some contemplative writers [. . .] appear to pull away from such a gaze with troubling quickness, their inspection transmogrifying into rumination on essence or the web of being or bolting into the language of piety and praise. Their looking seems not wild and helpless enough, seems too nicely contained in understanding; it travels into the world only far enough to grasp the presence it anticipates; it appears to lack the terror of ecstasy. If you look hard enough at the world, past a region of comprehension surrounding things, you enter a vast unusualness that defeats you. You do not arrive at a name or a home. Look at a meadow long enough and your bearings vanish. The world seen deeply eludes all names; it is not like anything; it is not the sign of something else. It is itself. It is a towering strangeness.

TIM LILBURN, *Living in the World as if It Were Home*

THE BENNETT SPRINGS ROAD

I knew it was there, if I'd had time to look:
the sweet water falling over rock,
the leaf-mold floor, secret to all but light,
the tall boles stationed between day and night.

This is the heart of the mountain, not the crest.
Season and century league in some high place,
impulsive powers that beat the peak to sand
and scatter Appalachian on the wind.

And lie at last by the little stream that brings
all gods to truth. On the road to Bennett Springs,
tired of the paltry ridges, I lay down
the last of my youth where all the gods had grown,
became the water falling over the stone,
became the forest-father to red men,
became the tribe of stars, both daughter and son,
the mother of moss, the bird that sang I am.

JULIA RANDALL

HOW STARS START

I don't ask to be forgiven
nor do I wish to be given up,
not entirely, not yet, not while
pain is shooting clean through
the only world I know: this one.
This is no Mal Waldron song or
Marlene Dietrich epic in black
& white where to scrawl against
the paradigms of time is to mean
something benign, like dismissing
present actions or behavior because
I know & understand deep down
inside & beyond that life itself
is acting all of this out; this
kamikaze drama, cosmic if you
will, but certainly comic, in a style
so common as to invite confusion.

Who am I now? What have I become?
Where do we draw the line between being
who I am and what I ought to be?
Need is a needle, nosing its sticky load
into my grief, spilling into veins
that can't be sewn, transforming their dark
cells in lighted semblances of relief.
The stomach is involved; flesh itself;
memories of an island doom that leaves
no room for sense or sensitive
assessments of truth about myself.
Which is the me that never changes?

All roads lead back to starts, to where
I started out, to stars: the fiery
beginnings of our ends & means; our
meanness & our meanings. There never
was a night begun in darkness,
nor a single day begun in light.

AL YOUNG

Often, during stressful times when I was small—while changing schools, when bullied or after my parents had argued—I'd lie in bed before I fell asleep and count in my head all the different layers between me and the center of the earth: crust, mantle, outer core, inner core. Then I'd think upward in expanding rings of thinning air: troposphere, stratosphere, mesosphere, thermosphere, exosphere. Miles beneath me was molten rock, miles above me limitless dust and vacancy, and there I'd lie with the warm blanket of the troposphere over me and a red cotton duvet cover too, and the smell of the night's dinner lingering upstairs, and downstairs the sound of my mother busy at her typewriter.

This evening ritual wasn't a test of how much I could keep in my mind at once, or of how far I could send my imagination. It had something of the power of incantation, but it did not seem a compulsion, and it was not a prayer. No matter how tightly the day's bad things had gripped me, there was so much up there above me, so much below, so many places and states that were implacable, unreachable, entirely uninterested in human affairs. Listing them one by one built imaginative sanctuary between walls of unknowing knowns. It helped in other ways too. Sleeping was like losing time, somehow like not being alive, and drifting into it at night there sometimes came a panic that I might not find my way back from wherever I had gone. My own private vespers felt a little like counting the steps up a flight of steep stairs. I needed to know where I was. It was a way of bringing me home.

HELEN MACDONALD, "THE MYSTERIOUS
LIFE OF BIRDS WHO NEVER COME DOWN"

Home indeed. For the natural world is where we evolved; where we became what we are, where we learned to feel and to react. It is where the human imagination formed and took flight, where it found its metaphors and its similes, among trees and pure rivers and wild creatures and grasslands rippled by the wind, and also among poisonous snakes and lethal predators and enemies and the unending quest for sustenance—but not among concrete buildings and automobiles and sewers and central heating and supermarkets, for these last are just accretions, add-ons which have been with us merely for the blink of an eye in evolutionary time, no matter how much they now may dominate our lives. Deep down, they mean nothing. It is nature which is the true haven for our psyches.

MICHAEL MCCARTHY, *The Moth Snowstorm: Nature and Joy*

THE EIGHTH ELEGY

Dedicated to Rudolf Kassner

With all its eyes the natural world looks out
into the Open. Only *our* eyes are turned
backward, and surround plant, animal, child
like traps, as they emerge into their freedom.
We know what is really out there only from
the animal's gaze; for we take the very young
child and force it around, so that it sees
objects—not the Open, which is so
deep in animals' faces. Free from death.
We, only, can see death; the free animal
has its decline in back of it, forever,
and God in front, and when it moves, it moves
already in eternity, like a fountain.
      Never, not for a single day, do *we* have
before us that pure space into which flowers
endlessly open. Always there is World
and never Nowhere without the No: that pure
unseparated element which one breathes
without desire and endlessly *knows*. A child
may wander there for hours, through the timeless
stillness, may get lost in it and be
shaken back. Or someone dies and *is* it.
For, nearing death, one doesn't see death; but stares
beyond, perhaps with an animal's vast gaze.
Lovers, if the beloved were not there
blocking the view, are close to it, and marvel . . .
As if by some mistake, it opens for them
behind each other . . . but neither can move past

the other, and it changes back to World.
Forever turned toward objects, we see in them
the mere reflection of the realm of freedom,
which we have dimmed. Or when some animal
mutely, serenely, looks us through and through.
That is what fate means: to be opposite,
to be opposite and nothing else, forever.

If the animal moving toward us so securely
in a different direction had our kind of
consciousness—, it would wrench us around and drag us
along its path. But it feels its life as boundless,
unfathomable, and without regard
to its own condition: pure, like its outward gaze.
And where we see the future, it sees all time
and itself within all time, forever healed.

Yet in the alert, warm animal there lies
the pain and burden of an enormous sadness.
For it too feels the presence of what often
overwhelms us: a memory, as if
the element we keep pressing toward was once
more intimate, more true, and our communion
infinitely tender. Here all is distance;
there it was breath. After that first home,
the second seems ambiguous and drafty.
    Oh bliss of the *tiny* creature which remains
forever inside the womb that was its shelter;
joy of the gnat which, still *within*, leaps up
even at its marriage: for everything is womb.

And look at the half-assurance of the bird,
which knows both inner and outer, from its source,
as if it were the soul of an Etruscan,
flown out of a dead man received inside a space,
but with his reclining image as the lid.
And how bewildered is any womb-born creature
that has to fly. As if terrified and fleeing
from itself, it zigzags through the air, the way
a crack runs through a teacup. So the bat
quivers across the porcelain of evening.

And we: spectators, always, everywhere,
turned toward the world of objects, never outward.
It fills us. We arrange it. It breaks down.
We rearrange it, then break down ourselves.

Who has twisted us around like this, so that
no matter what we do, we are in the posture
of someone going away? Just as, upon
the farthest hill, which shows him his whole valley
one last time, he turns, stops, lingers—,
so we live here, forever taking leave.

RAINER MARIA RILKE

(TRANSLATED FROM THE GERMAN

BY STEPHEN MITCHELL)

LOT'S WIFE

The just man followed then his angel guide
Where he strode on the black highway, hulking and bright;
But a wild grief in his wife's bosom cried,
Look back, it is not too late for a last sight

Of the red towers of your native Sodom, the square
Where once you sang, the gardens you shall mourn,
And the tall house with empty windows where
You loved your husband and your babes were born.

She turned, and looking on the bitter view
Her eyes were welded shut by mortal pain;
Into transparent salt her body grew,
And her quick feet were rooted in the plain.

Who would waste tears upon her? Is she not
The least of our losses, this unhappy wife?
Yet in my heart she will not be forgot
Who, for a single glance, gave up her life.

ANNA AKHMATOVA

(TRANSLATED FROM THE RUSSIAN

BY RICHARD WILBUR)

Imagine a Carthage sown with salt, and all the sowers gone, and the seeds lain however long in the earth, till there rose finally in vegetable profusion leaves and trees of rime and brine. What flowering would there be in such a garden? Light would force each salt calyx to open in prisms, and to fruit heavily with bright globes of water— peaches and grapes are little more than that, and where the world was salt there would be greater need of slaking. For need can blossom into all the compensations it requires. To crave and to have are as like as a thing and its shadow. For when does a berry break upon the tongue as sweetly as when one longs to taste it, and when is the taste refracted into so many hues and savors of ripeness and earth, and when do our senses know any thing so utterly as when we lack it? And here again is a foreshadowing—the world will be made whole. For to wish for a hand on one's hair is all but to feel it. So whatever we may lose, very craving gives it back to us again. Though we dream and hardly know it, longing, like an angel, fosters us, smooths our hair, and brings us wild strawberries. . . .

If there had been snow I would have made a statue, a woman to stand along the path, among the trees. The children would have come close, to look at her. Lot's wife was salt and barren, because she was full of loss and mourning, and looked back. But here rare flowers would gleam in her hair, and on her breast, and in her hands, and there would be children all around her, to love and marvel at her for her beauty, and to laugh at her extravagant adornments, as if they had set the flowers in her hair and thrown down all the flowers at her feet, and they would forgive her, eagerly and lavishly, for turning away, though she never asked to be forgiven. Though her hands were ice and did not touch them, she would be more than mother to them, she so calm, so still, and they such wild and orphan things.

MARILYNNE ROBINSON, *Housekeeping*

ODE TO THE HOTEL NEAR
THE CHILDREN'S HOSPITAL

Praise the restless beds
Praise the beds that do not adjust
    that won't lift the head to feed
    or lower for shots
    or blood
    or raise to watch the tinny TV
Praise the hotel TV that won't quit
    its murmur & holler
Praise visiting hours
Praise the room service
    that doesn't exist
    just the slow delivery to the front desk
    of cooling pizzas
    & brown bags leaky
    greasy & clear
Praise the vending machines
Praise the change
Praise the hot water
& the heat
    or the loud cool
    that helps the helpless sleep.

Praise the front desk
    who knows to wake
    Rm 120 when the hospital rings
Praise the silent phone
Praise the dark drawn
    by thick daytime curtains
    after long nights of waiting,
    awake.

Praise the waiting & then praise the nothing
    that's better than bad news
Praise the wakeup call
    at 6am
Praise the sleeping in
Praise the card hung on the door
    like a whisper
    lips pressed silent
Praise the stranger's hands
    that change the sweat of sheets
Praise the checking out

Praise the going home
    to beds unmade
    for days
Beds that won't resurrect
    or rise
that lie there like a child should
        sleeping, tubeless

Praise this mess
    that can be left

KEVIN YOUNG

SPARROW TRAPPED IN THE AIRPORT

Never the bark and abalone mask
Cracked by storms of a mastering god,
Never the gods' favored glamour, never
The pelagic messenger bearing orchards
In its beak, never allegory, not wisdom
Or valor or cunning, much less hunger
Demanding vigilance, industry, invention,
Or the instinct to claim some small rise
Above the plain and from there to assert
The song of another day ending;
Lentil-brown, uncounted, overlooked
In the clamorous public of the flock
So unlikely to be noticed here by arrivals,
Faces shining with oils of their many miles,
Where it hops and scratches below
The baggage carousel and lights too high,
Too bright for any real illumination,
Looking more like a fumbled punch line
Than a stowaway whose revelation
Recalls how lightly we once traveled.

AVERILL CURDY

You God cannot be God unless we create a dwelling place for you in our hearts.

ETTY HILLESUM, *An Interrupted Life*

PRAYER

Some days, although we cannot pray, a prayer
utters itself. So, a woman will lift
her head from the sieve of her hands and stare
at the minims sung by a tree, a sudden gift.

Some nights, although we are faithless, the truth
enters our hearts, that small familiar pain;
then a man will stand stock-still, hearing his youth
in the distant Latin chanting of a train.

Pray for us now. Grade I piano scales
console the lodger looking out across
a Midlands town. Then dusk, and someone calls
a child's name as though they named their loss.

Darkness outside. Inside, the radio's prayer—
Rockall. Malin. Dogger. Finisterre.

CAROL ANN DUFFY

from CHORUSES FROM "THE ROCK"

We build in vain unless the LORD build with us.
Can you keep the City that the LORD keeps not with you?
A thousand policemen directing the traffic
Cannot tell you why you come or where you go.
A colony of cavies or a horde of active marmots
Build better than they that build without the LORD.
Shall we lift up our feet among perpetual ruins?
I have loved the beauty of Thy House, the peace of Thy sanctuary,
I have swept the floors and garnished the altars.
Where there is no temple there shall be no homes,
Though you have shelters and institutions,
Precarious lodgings while the rent is paid,
Subsiding basements where the rat breeds
Or sanitary dwellings with numbered doors
Or a house a little better than your neighbour's;
When the Stranger says: "What is the meaning of this city?
Do you huddle close together because you love each other?"
What will you answer? "We all dwell together
To make money from each other"? or "This is a community"?
And the Stranger will depart and return to the desert.
O my soul, be prepared for the coming of the Stranger,
Be prepared for him who knows how to ask questions.

    O weariness of men who turn from GOD
To the grandeur of your mind and the glory of your action,
To arts and inventions and daring enterprises,
To schemes of human greatness thoroughly discredited,
Binding the earth and the water to your service,
Exploiting the seas and developing the mountains,
Dividing the stars into common and preferred,

Engaged in devising the perfect refrigerator,
Engaged in working out a rational morality,
Engaged in printing as many books as possible,
Plotting of happiness and flinging empty bottles,
Turning from your vacancy to fevered enthusiasm
For nation or race or what you call humanity;
Though you forget the way to the Temple,
There is one who remembers the way to your door:
Life you may evade, but Death you shall not.
You shall not deny the Stranger.

T. S. ELIOT

SNAKE

A snake came to my water-trough
On a hot, hot day, and I in pyjamas for the heat,
To drink there.

In the deep, strange-scented shade of the great dark carob tree
I came down the steps with my pitcher
And must wait, must stand and wait, for there he was at the trough
    before me.

He reached down from a fissure in the earth-wall in the gloom
And trailed his yellow-brown slackness soft-bellied down, over
    the edge of the stone trough
And rested his throat upon the stone bottom,
And where the water had dripped from the tap, in a small clearness,
He sipped with his straight mouth,
Softly drank through his straight gums, into his slack long body,
Silently.

Someone was before me at my water-trough,
And I, like a second-comer, waiting.

He lifted his head from his drinking, as cattle do,
And looked at me vaguely, as drinking cattle do,
And flickered his two-forked tongue from his lips, and mused
    a moment,
And stooped and drank a little more,
Being earth-brown, earth-golden from the burning bowels
    of the earth
On the day of Sicilian July, with Etna smoking.

The voice of my education said to me
He must be killed,
For in Sicily the black, black snakes are innocent, the gold
    are venomous.

And voices in me said, If you were a man
You would take a stick and break him now, and finish him off.

But must I confess how I liked him,
How glad I was he had come like a guest in quiet, to drink
    at my water-trough
And depart peaceful, pacified, and thankless,
Into the burning bowels of this earth?

Was it cowardice, that I dared not kill him?
Was it perversity, that I longed to talk to him?
Was it humility, to feel so honoured?
I felt so honoured.

And yet those voices:
If you were not afraid, you would kill him!

And truly I was afraid, I was most afraid,
But even so, honoured still more
That he should seek my hospitality
From out the dark door of the secret earth.

He drank enough
And lifted his head, dreamily, as one who has drunken,
And flickered his tongue like a forked night on the air, so black,

Seeming to lick his lips,
And looked around like a god, unseeing, into the air,
And slowly turned his head,
And slowly, very slowly, as if thrice adream,
Proceeded to draw his slow length curving round
And climb again the broken bank of my wall-face.

And as he put his head into that dreadful hole,
And as he slowly drew up, snake-easing his shoulders,
        and entered farther,
A sort of horror, a sort of protest against his withdrawing into
        that horrid black hole,
Deliberately going into the blackness, and slowly drawing
        himself after,
Overcame me now his back was turned.

I looked round, I put down my pitcher,
I picked up a clumsy log
And threw it at the water-trough with a clatter.

I think it did not hit him,
But suddenly that part of him that was left behind convulsed
        in an undignified haste,
Writhed like lightning, and was gone
Into the black hole, the earth-lipped fissure in the wall-front,
At which, in the intense still noon, I stared with fascination.

And immediately I regretted it.
I thought how paltry, how vulgar, what a mean act!
I despised myself and the voices of my accursed human education.

And I thought of the albatross,
And I wished he would come back, my snake.

For he seemed to me again like a king,
Like a king in exile, uncrowned in the underworld,
Now due to be crowned again.

And so, I missed my chance with one of the lords
Of life.
And I have something to expiate:
A pettiness.

D. H. LAWRENCE

So little lies between you and the earth and the sky. One look & you know that simply to survive every possible ally is needed—even most humble insect or reptile. You realize you will be speaking with all of them if you intend to last out the year.

LESLIE MARMON SILKO, Yellow Woman and a Beauty of the Spirit

To approach the Other in conversation is to welcome his expression, in which at each instant he overflows the idea a thought would carry away from it. It is therefore to receive from the Other beyond the capacity of the I, which means exactly: to have the idea of infinity. But this also means: to be taught.

EMMANUEL LEVINAS, Totality and Infinity: An Essay on Exteriority

GRACE

for Darlene Wind and James Welch

I think of Wind and her wild ways the year we had nothing to lose
and lost it anyway in the cursed country of the fox. We still talk
about that winter, how the cold froze imaginary buffalo on the
stuffed horizon of snowbanks. The haunting voices of the starved
and mutilated broke fences, crashed our thermostat dreams, and we
couldn't stand it one more time. So once again we lost a winter in
stubborn memory, walked through cheap apartment walls, skated
through fields of ghosts into a town that never wanted us, in the epic
search for grace.

Like Coyote, like Rabbit, we could not contain our terror and
clowned our way through a season of false midnights. We had
to swallow that town with laughter, so it would go down easy as
honey. And one morning as the sun struggled to break ice, and our
dreams had found us with coffee and pancakes in a truck stop along
Highway 80, we found grace.

I could say grace was a woman with time on her hands, or a white
buffalo escaped from memory. But in that dingy light it was a
promise of balance. We once again understood the talk of animals,
and spring was lean and hungry with the hope of children and corn.

I would like to say, with grace, we picked ourselves up and walked
into the spring thaw. We didn't; the next season was worse. You
went home to Leech Lake to work with the tribe and I went south.
And, Wind, I am still crazy. I know there is something larger than
the memory of a dispossessed people. We have seen it.

JOY HARJO

What is common to all indigenous peoples is a belief that we are all relatives, all being. All is sacred. I have been given glimpses of what some call the "everlasting." I have seen this place in a newborn's eyes, in sunrise, in dusk, the darkest night, and the face of a flower— here and in dreaming. The everlasting is who we truly are, where we truly belong. It is the stuff of poetry, music, and dance, of all arts. In this place, we are one person, one poem, one story, and one song.

JOY HARJO, *A God in the House*

SEABIRD'S BLESSING

We are crowds of seabirds,
makers of many angles,
workers that unpick a web
of the air's threads and tangles.

Pray for us when we fight
the wind one to one;
let not that shuddering strength
smash the cross of the wing-bone.

O God the featherer,
lift us if we fall;
preserve the frenzy in our mouths,
the yellow star in the eyeball.

Christ, make smooth the way
of a creature like a spirit
up from its perverse body
without weight or limit.

Holy ghost of heaven,
blow us clear of the world,
give us the utmost of the air
to heave on and to hold.

Pray for us this weird
bare place—we are screaming
O sky count us not as nothing
O sea count us not as nothing

ALICE OSWALD

THE SOUND OF TREES

I wonder about the trees.
Why do we wish to bear
Forever the noise of these
More than another noise
So close to our dwelling place?
We suffer them by the day
Till we lose all measure of pace,
And fixity in our joys,
And acquire a listening air.
They are that that talks of going
But never gets away;
And that talks no less for knowing,
As it grows wiser and older,
That now it means to stay.
My feet tug at the floor
And my head sways to my shoulder
Sometimes when I watch trees sway,
From the window or the door.
I shall set forth for somewhere,
I shall make the reckless choice
Some day when they are in voice
And tossing so as to scare
The white clouds over them on.
I shall have less to say,
But I shall be gone.

ROBERT FROST

Trees are sanctuaries. Whoever knows how to speak to them, whoever knows how to listen to them, can learn the truth. They do not preach learning and precepts, they preach, undeterred by particulars, the ancient law of life.

A tree says: A kernel is hidden in me, a spark, a thought, I am life from eternal life. The attempt and the risk that the eternal mother took with me is unique, unique the form and veins of my skin, unique the smallest play of leaves in my branches and the smallest scar on my bark. I was made to form and reveal the eternal in my smallest special detail.

A tree says: My strength is trust. I know nothing about my fathers, I know nothing about the thousand children that every year spring out of me. I live out the secret of my seed to the very end, and I care for nothing else. I trust that God is in me. I trust that my labor is holy. Out of this trust I live.

When we are stricken and cannot bear our lives any longer, then a tree has something to say to us: Be still! Be still! Look at me! Life is not easy, life is not difficult. Those are childish thoughts . . . Home is neither here nor there. Home is within you, or home is nowhere at all.

A longing to wander tears my heart when I hear trees rustling in the wind at evening. If one listens to them silently for a long time, this longing reveals its kernel, its meaning. It is not so much a matter of escaping from one's suffering, though it may seem to be so. It is a longing for home, for a memory of the mother, for new metaphors for life. It leads home. Every path leads homeward, every step is birth, every step is death, every grave is mother.

HERMAN HESSE, *Wandering: Notes and Sketches*

FAMILY PRIME

Our golden age was then, when lamp and rug
Were one and warm, were globe against the indifferent
Million of cold things a world contains.
None there. A light shone inward, shutting out
All that was not corn yellow and love young.

Like winter bears we moved, our minds, our bodies
Jointed to fit the roundness of a room:
As sluggish, and as graceful, whether couch
Or table intercepted, or if marbles
Clicked on the floor and hunched us into play.

How long? I do not know. Before, a blank.
And after, all this oldness, them and me,
With the wind slicing in from everywhere,
And figures growing small. I may remember
Only a month of this. Or a God's hour.

Yet I remember, and my father said
He did: the moment spherical, that age
Fixes and gilds; eternity one evening
Perfect, such as maybe my own sons,
And yours, will know the taste of in their time.

MARK VAN DOREN

For all that, people still persist in thinking that *life is flat* and runs from birth to death. But life, too, is probably round, and much greater in scope and possibilities than the hemisphere we now know.

VINCENT VAN GOGH, LETTER TO ÉMILE BERNARD

Poetry gives not so much a nostalgia for youth, which would be vulgar, as a nostalgia for the expressions of youth. It offers us images as we should have imagined them during the "original impulse" of youth. Primal images, simple engravings are but so many invitations to start imagining again. They give us back areas of being, houses in which the human being's certainty of being is concentrated, and we have the impression that, by living in such images as these, in images that are as stabilizing as these are, we could start a new life, a life that would be our own, that would belong to us in our very depths.

GASTON BACHELARD, *The Poetics of Space*

from GLANMORE SONNETS

I used to lie with an ear to the line
For that way, they said, there should come a sound
Escaping ahead, an iron tune
Of flange and piston pitched along the ground,
But I never heard that. Always, instead,
Struck couplings and shuntings two miles away
Lifted over the woods. The head
Of a horse swirled back from a gate, a grey
Turnover of haunch and mane, and I'd look
Up to the cutting where she'd soon appear.
Two fields back, in the house, small ripples shook
Silently across our drinking water
(As they are shaking now across my heart)
And vanished into where they seemed to start.

SEAMUS HEANEY

When I first encountered the name of the city of Stockholm, I little thought that I would ever visit it, never mind end up being welcomed to it as a guest of the Swedish Academy and the Nobel Foundation. At the time I am thinking of, such an outcome was not just beyond expectation: it was simply beyond conception. In the nineteen forties, when I was the eldest child of an ever-growing family in rural Co. Derry, we crowded together in the three rooms of a traditional thatched farmstead and lived a kind of den-life which was more or less emotionally and intellectually proofed against the outside world. It was an intimate, physical, creaturely existence in which the night sounds of the horse in the stable beyond one bedroom wall mingled with the sounds of adult conversation from the kitchen beyond the other. We took in everything that was going on, of course—rain in the trees, mice on the ceiling, a steam train rumbling along the railway line one field back from the house—but we took it in as if we were in the doze of hibernation. Ahistorical, pre-sexual, in suspension between the archaic and the modern, we were as susceptible and impressionable as the drinking water that stood in a bucket in our scullery: every time a passing train made the earth shake, the surface of that water used to ripple delicately, concentrically, and in utter silence. . . .

I credit poetry for making this space-walk possible. I credit it immediately because of a line I wrote fairly recently instructing myself (and whoever else might be listening) to "walk on air against your better judgement." But I credit it ultimately because poetry can make an order as true to the impact of external reality and as sensitive to the inner laws of the poet's being as the ripples that rippled in and rippled out across the water in that scullery bucket fifty years ago. An order where we can at last grow up to that which we stored up as we grew. An order which satisfies all that is appetitive in the intelligence and prehensile in the affections. I credit poetry, in other words, both for being itself and for being a help, for making possible a fluid and restorative relationship between the mind's centre and its circumference, between the child gazing at the word "Stockholm" on the face of the radio dial and the man facing the faces that he meets in Stockholm at this most privileged moment. I credit it because credit is due to it, in our time and in all time, for its truth to life, in every sense of that phrase.

SEAMUS HEANEY, "CREDITING POETRY"

AFTER MAKING LOVE WE HEAR FOOTSTEPS

For I can snore like a bullhorn
or play loud music
or sit up talking with any reasonably sober Irishman
and Fergus will only sink deeper
into his dreamless sleep, which goes by all in one flash,
but let there be that heavy breathing
or a stifled come-cry anywhere in the house
and he will wrench himself awake
and make for it on the run—as now, we lie together,
after making love, quiet, touching along the length of our bodies,
familiar touch of the long-married,
and he appears—in his baseball pajamas, it happens,
the neck opening so small he has to screw them on—
and flops down between us and hugs us and snuggles himself to sleep,
his face gleaming with satisfaction at being this very child.

In the half darkness we look at each other
and smile
and touch arms across this little, startlingly muscled body—
this one whom habit of memory propels to the ground of his making,
sleeper only the mortal sounds can sing awake,
this blessing love gives again into our arms.

GALWAY KINNELL

HOMELAND SECURITY

The four a.m. cries
of my son worm
through the double
foam of earplugs

and diazepam.
The smoke alarm's
green eye glows.
Beneath the cries,

the squirm and bristle
of the night's catch
of fiddlebacks
on the glue-traps

guarding our bed.
Necrotic music.
Scored in my head.
And all night columns

of ants have tramped
through the ruins
of my sleep, bearing
the fipronil

I left for them
home to their queen.
Patriot ants.
Out of republics

endlessly perishing.
If I can hold
out long enough,
maybe my wife

will go. If she
waits long enough,
maybe he'll go back
down on his own.

GEOFFREY BROCK

HOME AGAIN, HOME AGAIN

The children are back, the children are back—
They've come to take refuge, exhale and unpack;
The marriage has faltered, the job has gone bad,
Come open the door for them, Mother and Dad.

The city apartment is leaky and cold,
The landlord lascivious, greedy and old—
The mattress is lumpy, the oven's encrusted,
The freezer, the fan, and the toilet have rusted.

The company caved, the boss went broke,
The job and the love affair, all up in smoke.
The anguish of loneliness comes as a shock—
O heart in the doldrums, O heart in hock.

And so they return with their piles of possessions,
Their terrified cats and their mournful expressions,
Reclaiming the bedrooms they had in their teens,
Clean towels, warm comforter, glass figurines.

Downstairs in the kitchen the father and mother
Don't say a word, but they look at each other
As down from the hill comes Jill, comes Jack.
The children are back. The children are back.

MARILYN L. TAYLOR

LIFE IS A CARNIVAL

Dinner finished, wine in hand, in a vaguely competitive spirit
of disclosure, we trail Google Earth's invisible pervert
through the streets of our hometowns, but find them shabbier, or
   grossly

contemporized, denuded of childhood's native flora,
stuccoed or in some other way hostile
to the historical reenactments we expect of our former

settings. What sadness in the disused curling rinks, their illegal
basement bars imploding, in the seed of a Walmart
sprouting in the demographic, in Street View's perpetual noon. With
   pale

and bloated production values, hits of AM radio rise
to the surface of a network of social relations long obsolete. We sense
a loss of rapport. But how sweet the persistence

of angle parking! Would we burn these places rather than see them
change, or simply burn them, the sites of wreckage
from which we staggered with our formative injuries into the rest

of our lives. They cannot be consigned to the fourfold,
though the age we were belongs to someone else. Like our old
house. Look what they've done to it. Who thought this would be fun?

A concert, then, YouTube from those inconceivable days before
YouTube, an era boarded over like a bankrupt country store,
cans still on its shelves, so hastily did we leave it. How beautiful

they are in their poncey clothes, their youthful higher
registers, fullscreen, two of them dead now. Is this
eternity? Encore, applause, encore; it's almost like being there.

KAREN SOLIE

It's one thing to develop a nostalgia for home while you're boozing with Yankee writers in Martha's Vineyard or being chased by the bulls in Pamplona. It's something else to go home and visit with the folks in Reed's drugstore on the square and actually listen to them. The reason you can't go home again is not because the down-home folks are mad at you—they're not, don't flatter yourself, they couldn't care less—but because once you're in orbit and you return to Reed's drugstore on the square, you can stand no more than fifteen minutes of the conversation before you head for the woods, head for the liquor store, or head back to Martha's Vineyard, where at least you can put a tolerable and saving distance between you and home. Home may be where the heart is but it's no place to spend Wednesday afternoon.

WALKER PERCY, *Lost in the Cosmos: The Last Self-Help Book*

Everyone needs a village, if only for the pleasure of leaving it.

CESARE PAVESE, *The Moon and the Bonfires*

Some people may think it was not the best place in the world for him to be brought up in; but it must have been, for there he was.

GEORGE MACDONALD, *At the Back of the North Wind*

EXODUS 10

There is nothing in the make-up of a Negro, physically or mentally,
which should induce anyone to welcome him as a neighbor. The best
of them are insanitary, insurance companies class them as poor risks,
ruin alone follows in their path.

(FROM A 1920 ISSUE OF THE *Property Owners' Journal*, 151)

And the Lord said unto the people,
"Stretch out thy hands toward heaven,
that there may be darkness over the city,
even darkness which may be felt."
And the people stretched forth their hands,
and there was a thick darkness in all the city:
it weighed heavy on the heads of saint
and sinner alike. And the people smiled upon the darkness,
and the darkness was good. For upon them the darkness
was as burnt sugar: pleasing to the skin, and sweet upon the lips.
And the people delighted in the darkness.
But upon the wicked, the darkness was as a plague,
and beneath it they writhed in torment, weeping and calling for mercy.
The thickness of the darkness was such that they saw not one another,
neither rose any from their place for days. And the people found leisure,
calling to one another through the darkness as in a child's game,
and they found each other in laughter. And to them, all noise was joyful
in the darkness, so that each found the work of the Lord
in the song of the sparrow or the sigh of a sleeping infant. And it
    was good.
But the wicked people were slothful, and found only misery in
    their repose.
And the kings, their hearts hardened, called unto the people, and said,
"Go! Get thee from us! Take heed to thyselves, and leave the city."

But the people stood in the darkness, and each reached with a staff
toward heaven, and they spoke as one, saying then "Nay,
for the Lord our God is with us, and the city is granted unto us,
and it shall be a city of darkness for all days to come."

EVE EWING

ODE TO GENTRIFICATION

Old school denizens of this
bleach-boned block say:
the realest thing
about the white woman
and her Yorkie
on this reimagined street
is the leather of the leash
that tethers them.

Your very name, glass
splinter planted deep in the fat
of our vernacular. Gentrification,
rightly mistaken
for juxtaposition:
pretty boys with swagger,
checkerboard trains,
skyscraper sadness,
bodegas sighing out soy.

Peruvian girl and boy fattening
fridges with Fiji between
homeworks, while Pops
slices and dices, and Mom
rocks the register.

Kissing cousin to gratification,
you birth gratitude—
twin to regret.
Call me *regrateful*.

I am so sorry to thank you
for the manner in which
I participate in your cruel,
and convenient, magic.

You ushered out
the families who dreamed
where my head now rests.

Yesterday, I retrieved laundry
cleaner than bells, unmentionables
caressed by another's
mother's hands.

I sit on the up-
side of your coin,
drinking down the sky's blue
dregs, while the teens I teach,
and the sturdy black
grandmothers I salute
with my seat,
kiss concrete.

SAMANTHA THORNHILL

THE LANDLADY

This is the lair of the landlady.

She is
a raw voice
loose in the rooms beneath me,

the continuous henyard
squabble going on below
thought in this house like
the bicker of blood through the head.

She is everywhere, intrusive as the smells
that bulge in under my doorsill;
she presides over my
meagre eating, generates
the light for eyestrain.

From her I rent my time:
she slams
my days like doors.
Nothing is mine

and when I dream images
of daring escapes through the snow
I find myself walking
always over a vast face
which is the land-
lady's, and wake up shouting.

She is a bulk, a knot
swollen in a space. Though I have tried

to find some way around
her, my senses
are cluttered by perception
and can't see through her.

She stands there, a raucous fact
blocking my way:
immutable, a slab
of what is real,

solid as bacon.

MARGARET ATWOOD

PERSONS FROM PORLOCK

Meals to be plied, fires to be bought,
You with your business at the hand
Talking away my thought
Where opium wined and dined,
How small you beer the mind!

How your clerk ways abolish
With a blue lead the murex hours,
How copy out in chores
The inimitable furniture, demolish
The castles in my airs!
I would shake out my casuistry, polish
My syntax, dust the chemistry of stars
To hitch my dactyls, darn
Achilles, turn a sheet of metaphors.

I talk in tons; you have me caught
To quibble at the figure of an ounce,
You comma in the general sense,
You dot above the art!
Then cross my needs and go,
Doffing your chat at the gate,
Taking your leave with well-fed words
As pied and appled as your portmanteau,
As neat as your regards,
As Porlock as your heart.

ROSAMUND STANHOPE

[WHAT HAPPINESS]

What happiness
In the building across the street from me and my dreams!

It's inhabited by people I don't know, whom I've seen but
    not seen.
They're happy, because they're not me.

The children who play on the high balconies
Live forever, without doubt,
Among flowerpots.

The voices rising from inside the homes
Always sing, without doubt.
Yes, they must sing.

When there's feasting out here, there's feasting in there,
Which is bound to be the case where everything's in
    agreement:
Man with Nature, because the city is Nature.

What tremendous happiness not to be me!

But don't others feel the same way?
What others? There are no others.
What others feel is a home with shut windows,
And when they're opened
It's for their children to play on the railed balcony,
Among the pots with I don't know what sort of flowers.

Other people never feel.
We're the ones who feel,

Yes, all of us,
Even I, who am now feeling nothing.

Nothing? Well . . .
A slight pain that's nothing . . .

ÁLVARO DE CAMPOS (FERNANDO PESSOA)

(TRANSLATED FROM THE PORTUGUESE

BY RICHARD ZENITH)

It is a joy to be hidden, and disaster not to be found.

D. W. WINNICOTT, *The Maturational Processes and the Facilitating Environment: Studies in the Theory of Emotional Development*

I LOVE THAT FIRST BUILDER

I love that first builder
who left a hole in the wall
—a small round hole,
or a square one—
for ventilation
or to look at the world from the inside.
When you're sheltered by walls
you can let your eyes roam beyond them
like a dog relieving itself.
I thought about leaving a window
in my body as well
so I could twist my neck
and look inwards, gaze
at my own heart
and ask myself:
Why is this man I love
crying like that, so much now
that he's soaking my soul?

GIHAN OMAR
(TRANSLATED FROM THE ARABIC
BY KAREEM JAMES ABU-ZEID)

And where are the windows? Where does the light come in? . . .
Maybe the light is going to have to come in as best it can, through
whatever chinks and cracks have been left in the builder's faulty
craftsmanship, and if that's the case you can be sure that nobody
feels worse about it than I do. God knows, Bernie; God knows there
certainly ought to be a window around here somewhere, for all of us.

RICHARD YATES, "BUILDERS"

THE STARE'S NEST BY MY WINDOW

The bees build in the crevices
Of loosening masonry, and there
The mother birds bring grubs and flies.
My wall is loosening; honey bees,
Come build in the empty house of the stare.

We are closed in, and the key is turned
On our uncertainty; somewhere
A man is killed, or a house burned,
Yet no clear fact to be discerned:
Come build in the empty house of the stare.

A barricade of stone or of wood;
Some fourteen days of civil war;
Last night they trundled down the road
That dead young soldier in his blood:
Come build in the empty house of the stare.

We had fed the heart on fantasies,
The heart's grown brutal from the fare;
More substance in our enmities
Than in our love; O honey-bees,
Come build in the empty house of the stare.

W. B. YEATS

TELL THE BEES

Tell the bees. They require news of the house;
they must know, lest they sicken
from the gap between their ignorance and our grief.
Speak in a whisper. Tie a black swatch
to a stick and attach the stick to their hive.
From the fortress of casseroles and desserts
built in the kitchen these past few weeks
as though hunger were the enemy, remove
a slice of cake and lay it where they can
slowly draw it in, making a mournful sound.

And tell the fly that has knocked on the window all day.
Tell the redbird that rammed the glass from outside
and stands too dazed to go. Tell the grass,
though it's already guessed, and the ground clenched in furrows;
tell the water you spill on the ground,
then all the water will know.
And the last shrunken pearl of snow in its hiding place.

Tell the blighted elms, and the young oaks we plant instead.
The water bug, while it scribbles
a hundred lines that dissolve behind it.
The lichen, while it etches deeper
its single rune. The boulders, letting their fissures widen,
the pebbles, which have no more to lose,
the hills—they will be slightly smaller, as always,

when the bees fly out tomorrow to look for sweetness
and find their way
because nothing else has changed.

SARAH LINDSAY

SEVEN LAMENTS FOR THE WAR-DEAD

1

Mr. Beringer, whose son
fell at the Canal that strangers dug
so ships could cross the desert,
crosses my path at Jaffa Gate.

He has grown very thin, has lost
the weight of his son.
That's why he floats so lightly in the alleys
and gets caught in my heart like little twigs
that drift away.

2

As a child he would mash his potatoes
to a golden mush.
And then you die.

A living child must be cleaned
when he comes home from playing.
But for a dead man
earth and sand are clear water, in which
his body goes on being bathed and purified
forever.

3

The Tomb of the Unknown Soldier
across there. On the enemy's side. A good landmark
for gunners of the future.

Or the war monument in London
at Hyde Park Corner, decorated
like a magnificent cake: yet another soldier
lifting head and rifle,
another cannon, another eagle, another
stone angel.

And the whipped cream of a huge marble flag
poured over it all
with an expert hand.

But the candied, much-too-red cherries
were already gobbled up
by the glutton of hearts. Amen.

4

I came upon an old zoology textbook,
Brehm, Volume II, *Birds:*
in sweet phrases, an account of the life of the starling,
swallow, and thrush. Full of mistakes in antiquated
Gothic typeface, but full of love, too. "Our feathered
friends." "Migrate from us to the warmer climes."
Nest, speckled egg, soft plumage, nightingale,
stork. "The harbingers of spring." The robin,
red-breasted.

Year of publication: 1913, Germany,
on the eve of the war that was to be
the eve of all my wars.

My good friend who died in my arms, in
his blood,
on the sands of Ashdod. 1948, June.

Oh my-friend,
red-breasted.

5

Dicky was hit.
Like the water tower at Yad Mordechai.
Hit. A hole in the belly. Everything
came flooding out.

But he has remained standing like that
in the landscape of my memory
like the water tower at Yad Mordechai.

He fell not far from there,
a little to the north, near Huleikat.

6

Is all of this
sorrow? I don't know.
I stood in the cemetery dressed in
the camouflage clothes of a living man: brown pants
and a shirt yellow as the sun.

Cemeteries are cheap; they don't ask for much.
Even the wastebaskets are small, made for holding

tissue paper
that wrapped flowers from the store.
Cemeteries are a polite and disciplined thing.
"I shall never forget you," in French
on a little ceramic plaque.
I don't know who it is that won't ever forget:
he's more anonymous than the one who died.

Is all of this sorrow? I guess so.
"May ye find consolation in the building
of the homeland." But how long
can you go on building the homeland
and not fall behind in the terrible
three-sided race
between consolation and building and death?

Yes, all of this is sorrow. But leave
a little love burning always
like the small bulb in the room of a sleeping baby
that gives him a bit of security and quiet love
though he doesn't know what the light is
or where it comes from.

7

Memorial Day for the war-dead: go tack on
the grief of all your losses—
including a woman who left you—
to the grief of losing them; go mix
one sorrow with another, like history,

that in its economical way
heaps pain and feast and sacrifice
onto a single day for easy reference.

Oh sweet world, soaked like bread
in sweet milk for the terrible
toothless God. "Behind all this,
some great happiness is hiding." No use
crying inside and screaming outside.
Behind all this, some great happiness may
be hiding.

Memorial day. Bitter salt, dressed up as
a little girl with flowers.
Ropes are strung out the whole length of the route
for a joint parade: the living and the dead together.
Children move with the footsteps of someone else's grief
as if picking their way through broken glass.

The flautist's mouth will stay pursed for many days.
A dead soldier swims among the small heads
with the swimming motions of the dead,
with the ancient error the dead have
about the place of the living water.

A flag loses contact with reality and flies away.
A store window decked out with beautiful dresses for women
in blue and white. And everything
in three languages: Hebrew, Arabic and Death.

A great royal beast has been dying all night long
under the jasmine,
with a fixed stare at the world.
A man whose son died in the war
walks up the street
like a woman with a dead fetus in her womb.
"Behind all this, some great happiness is hiding."

YEHUDA AMICHAI

(TRANSLATED FROM THE HEBREW

BY CHANA BLOCH)

No one today is purely one thing. Labels like Indian, or woman, or Muslim, or American are not more than starting-points, which if followed into actual experience for only a moment are quickly left behind. Imperialism consolidated the mixture of cultures and identities on a global scale. But its worst and most paradoxical gift was to allow people to believe that they were only, mainly, exclusively, white, or Black, or Western, or Oriental. Yet just as human beings make their own history, they also make their cultures and ethnic identities. No one can deny the persisting continuities of long traditions, sustained habitations, national languages, and cultural geographies, but there seems no reason except fear and prejudice to keep insisting on their separation and distinctiveness, as if that was all human life was about. Survival in fact is about the connections between things; in Eliot's phrase, reality cannot be deprived of the "other echoes [that] inhabit the garden."

EDWARD SAID, *Culture and Imperialism*

from SUMMER, SOMEWHERE

somewhere, a sun. below, boys brown
as rye play the dozens & ball, jump

in the air & stay there. boys become new
moons, gum-dark on all sides, beg bruise

-blue water to fly, at least tide, at least
spit back a father or two. I won't get started.

history is what it is. it knows what it did.
bad dog. bad blood. bad day to be a boy

color of a July well spent. but here, not earth
not heaven, we can't recall our white shirts

turned ruby gowns. here, there's no language
for *officer* or *law,* no color to call *white.*

if snow fell, it'd fall black. please, don't call
us dead, call us alive someplace better.

we say our own names when we pray.
we go out for sweets & come back.

DANEZ SMITH

IN A TIME OF PEACE

Inhabitant of earth for fortysomething years
I once found myself in a peaceful country. I watch neighbors open

their phones to watch
a cop demanding a man's driver's license. When the man reaches for
    his wallet, the cop
shoots. Into the car window. Shoots.

It is a peaceful country.

We pocket our phones and go.
To the dentist,
pick up the kids from school,
to buy shampoo
and basil.

Ours is a country in which a boy shot by police lies on the pavement
for hours.

We see in his open mouth
the nakedness
of the whole nation.

We watch. Watch
others watch.

The body of a boy lies on the pavement exactly like the body of a boy—

It is a peaceful country.

And it clips our citizens' bodies
effortlessly, the way the President's wife trims her toenails.

All of us
still have to do the hard work of dentist appointments,
of remembering to make
a summer salad: basil, tomatoes, it is a joy, tomatoes, add a little
    salt.

This is a time of peace.

I do not hear gunshots,
but watch birds splash over the backyards of the suburbs. How
    bright is the sky
as the avenue spins on its axis.
How bright is the sky (forgive me) how bright.

ILYA KAMINSKY

ITHAKA

As you set out for Ithaka
hope your road is a long one,
full of adventure, full of discovery.
Laistrygonians and Cyclops,
angry Poseidon—don't be afraid of them:
you'll never find things like that on your way
as long as you keep your thoughts raised high,
as long as a rare excitement
stirs your spirit and your body.
Laistrygonians and Cyclops,
wild Poseidon—you won't encounter them
unless you bring them along inside your soul,
unless your soul sets them up in front of you.

Hope the voyage is a long one.
May there be many a summer morning when,
with what pleasure, what joy,
you come into harbors seen for the first time;
may you stop at Phoenician trading stations
to buy fine things,
mother of pearl and coral, amber and ebony,
sensual perfume of every kind—
as many sensual perfumes as you can;
and may you visit many Egyptian cities
to gather stores of knowledge from their scholars.

Keep Ithaka always in your mind.
Arriving there is what you are destined for.
But do not hurry the journey at all.
Better if it lasts for years,

so you are old by the time you reach the island,
wealthy with all you have gained on the way,
not expecting Ithaka to make you rich.

Ithaka gave you the marvelous journey.
Without her you wouldn't have set out.
She has nothing left to give you now.

And if you find her poor, Ithaka won't have fooled you.
Wise as you will have become, so full of experience,
you will have understood by then what these Ithakas mean.

C. P. CAVAFY

(TRANSLATED FROM THE GREEK BY

EDMUND KEELEY)

WE WILL RISE

We will rise again beneath the walls of Knossos
And in Delphi the centre of the world
We will rise again in the harsh light of Crete

We will rise where words
Are the names of things
Where outlines are clear and vivid
There in the sharp light of Crete

We will rise where stone the stars and time
Are the kingdom of man
We will rise to stare straight at the earth
In the clean light of Crete

For it is good to clarify the heart of man
And to lift the black exactness of the cross
In the white light of Crete

SOPHIA DE MELLO BREYNER ANDRESEN

(TRANSLATED FROM THE PORTUGUESE

BY RICHARD ZENITH)

HARBOUR

But the sea was measured
and chained to the earth.
And the earth was measured
and chained to the sea.

They launched
cranes, lean angels,
they calculated
the wail of widowed sirens,
they foresaw
the nervous unrest of buoys,
they drafted
the labyrinth of routes around the world.

They constructed
the Minotaurs of ships.

They discovered five continents.

The earth was measured
and chained to the sea.
And the sea was measured
and chained to the earth.

All that is left
is a small house above the canal.
A man who spoke softly,
a woman with tears in her eyes.
All that is left is the evening lamp,

the continent of the table,
the tablecloth, a sea-gull that does not fly away.

All that is left
is a cup of tea,
the deepest ocean in the world.

MIROSLAV HOLUB

(TRANSLATED FROM THE CZECH BY

IAN MILNER AND GEORGE THEINER)

Back once again to the dust and patchwork construction, the exposed plastic pipes, raised tones, and weary hostility of our once Palestinian, now North African Jewish and increasingly ultra-Orthodox Jerusalem neighborhood, and to the grime of the run-down, battered, and tchotchke-crammed center of the city. Are its edges getting rougher or is all this time in New Haven each year thinning our skin? Then a call from a friend, and A. and I walk up several hills to a tidier and more genteel part of town: rose-filled gardens and geranium-studded municipal squares, sculptures, tree-lined streets, an early evening breeze. As though we'd crossed into Europe.

Each time we shift sides of the globe, or even sides of the city, the systole and diastole of belonging and dispersion leaves me a little dizzy, and melancholy. For some three decades now I've felt almost at home in exile and somehow in exile at home—though which is which is always evolving. And as in homes, so in poems. The heart is twisted back and forth, as if in some sort of rinse cycle, and maybe that's how it should be. This isn't just a slippery metaphysics to keep one's wings from being pinned down. It gets at something essential, perhaps what the philo-Semitic French Catholic poet Charles Péguy understood when he called "[being] elsewhere—the great vice of this race, its great and secret virtue, the great vocation of this people," the Jews. That doesn't sanction lack of attachment; it calls on us to be where we are and then some.

Tsvetaeva to the rescue again—"All poets are Jews"?

PETER COLE, *Hymns and Qualms*

(VALENT)LINES FOR A.

What law and power has blessed me so
that in this provocation of flesh
    I have been wedded to gentleness?
       *

Delicacy of an intricate
mesh of our thought and meals and talking
    has brought me to this exaltation

of syllables and a speechlessness—
to December dusk, and desk, and skin
    in the amber of our listening.
       *

Dawn again pink with munificence;
heart again blurred by its ignorance:
    toward you in that equation I turn—

and you, in turn, involve our being
spun like wool from which soul is weaving
    a use for that useless opulence.
       *

Doing and making—the end served by
what it is we make, and what we do,
    is what has made me: making and you.

PETER COLE

AN OLD-FASHIONED TRAVELLER ON THE TRADE ROUTES

I was sitting upstairs in a bus, cursing the waste of time, and pouring my life away on one of those insane journeys across London—while gradually the wavering motion of this precarious glass salon, that flung us about softly like trusses of wheat or Judo Lords, began its medicinal work inside the magnetic landscape of London.

The bus, with its transparent decks of people, trembled. And was as uniquely ceremonious in propelling itself as an eminent Jellyfish with an iron will, by expulsions, valves, hisses, steams, and emotional respirations. A militant, elementary, caparisoned Jellyfish, of the feminine sex, systematically eating and drinking the sea.

I began to feel as battered as though I had been making love all night! My limbs distilled the same interesting wide-awake weariness.

We went forward at a swimmer's pace, gazing through the walls that rocked the weather about like a cloudy drink from a chemist's shop—with the depth and sting of the Baltic. The air-shocks, the sulphur dioxides, the gelatin ignitions! We were all of us parcelled up in mud-coloured clothes, dreaming, while the rich perishable ensemble—as stuffy and exclusive as a bag of fish and chips, or as an Eskimo's bed in a glass drift—cautiously advanced as though on an exercise from a naval college.

The jogging was consistently idiotic, it induced a feeling of complete security. I gave up my complicated life on the spot; and lay screwed up like an old handkerchief screwed up in a pocket, suspended in time, ready to go to the ends of the earth. O trans-Siberian railways! Balloons! Astronauts!

ROSEMARY TONKS

BOHEMIA LIES BY THE SEA

If houses here are green, I'll step inside a house.
If bridges here are sound, I'll walk on solid ground.
If love's labour's lost in every age, I'll gladly lose it here.

If it's not me, it's one who is as good as me.

If a word here borders on me, I'll let it border.
If Bohemia still lies by the sea, I'll believe in the sea again.
And believing in the sea, thus I can hope for land.

If it's me, then it's anyone, for he's as worthy as me.
I want nothing more for myself. I want to go under.

Under—that means the sea, there I'll find Bohemia again.
From my grave, I wake in peace.
From deep down I know now, and I'm not lost.

Come here, all you Bohemians, seafarers, dock whores, and ships
unanchored. Don't you want to be Bohemians, all you Illyrians,
Veronese and Venetians. Play the comedies that make us laugh

until we cry. And err a hundred times,
as I erred and never withstood the trials,
though I did withstand them time after time.

As Bohemia withstood them and one fine day
was released to the sea and now lies by water.

I still border on a word and on another land,
I border, like little else, on everything more and more,

a Bohemian, a wandering minstrel, who has nothing, who
is held by nothing, gifted only at seeing, by a doubtful sea,
    the land of my choice.

INGEBORG BACHMANN

(TRANSLATED FROM THE GERMAN

BY PETER FILKINS)

We must take the feeling of being at home into exile. We must be rooted in the absence of a place.

SIMONE WEIL, *Gravity and Grace*

36

How deeply I drink up home-catalogs day—
they shine open my diorama and teach me
to lift my tiny arms to hang the dime
as a mirrory thing upon my shoebox wall.

Here's a sunshine page that reads,
"A home expands via the wise use of mirrors
wherever you wish a window."
I've read it all, I've read, I've read so much more

than I can withstand. A home expands via the you and I—
until then, dearest dime with my spit shined,
I will lift you up, I shall—I do—
"attend to what you do not have

and thereby," thereby. Thereby
make a home.

37

Over my home I rise on a trembling
wood-and-rope bridge. Sundown comes
in light-light red, lamps hung now in my hair
alight one question into the air:

Home, I made you best I could,
please don't break again beneath me?
I beat heavily upon my life until it gave.
As for prices, I've paid and paid.

All the while I cut the tiniest chairs,
a thimble ship, rice-paper walls
and Japanese fans cut from receipts
no wider than a little girl's nail.

Upon them I drew hills of wild plum, then
a hover of birds.

38

It was the constancy of birds
I heavy leaned upon. I'll risk you
not believing to tell a little truth: I rely upon
their whereabout sound right now.

No one coming for me, I could rot here in days.
I know Simone says forge a home in the void,
it's the void wherein roams the battered
kingdom, though she wouldn't use that word,

and neither would I except it came to me
as a strange feeling at my door to show the stones
its pockets bore, to sit and tell it was once
just a word for no, some spit in the face of lords.

No matter how we try, we're no good in the void.
Not the kingdom, not I, so birds, constancies, stay,

39

stay a spell in my persimmon tree.
I'm hefting myself up so many vacancies

might quiet in your perfect neutrality.
No contingency between us, no. Intimacy

is no promise but that we're alive a little together.
At dawn you undo my bedroom silence
and my emptiness isn't,
is not all mine to tend.

It's not traceable,
but to feel its radiance
maybe is all, maybe is everything—
maybe then arrives

the dying that breaks forth, can break open,
can break your life, it will break you

                    until you remain.

KATIE FORD

OLD MAMA SATURDAY

(*"Saturday's child must work for a living"*)

"I'm moving from Grief Street.
Taxes are high here
though the mortgage's cheap.

The house is well built.
With stuff to protect, that
mattered to me,
the security.

These things that I mind,
you know, aren't mine.
I mind minding them.
They weigh on my mind.

I don't mind them well.
I haven't got the knack
of kindly minding.
I say Take them back
but you never do.

When I throw them out
it may frighten you
and maybe me too.

       Maybe
it will empty me
too emptily

and keep me here
asleep, at sea
under the guilt quilt,
under the you tree."

MARIE PONSOT

POET'S WORK

Grandfather
  advised me:
    Learn a trade

I learned
  to sit at desk
    and condense

No layoff
  from this
    condensery
*
Property is poverty—
I've foreclosed.
I own again

these walls thin
as the back
of my writing tablet.

And more:
all who live here—
card table to eat on,

broken bed—
sacrifice for less
than art.
*
Now in one year
    a book published

           and plumbing—
took a lifetime
    to weep
           a deep
               trickle

                                    LORINE NIEDECKER

SILENCE

My father used to say,
"Superior people never make long visits,
have to be shown Longfellow's grave
or the glass flowers at Harvard.
Self-reliant like the cat—
that takes its prey to privacy,
the mouse's limp tail hanging like a shoelace from its mouth—
they sometimes enjoy solitude,
and can be robbed of speech
by speech which has delighted them.
The deepest feeling always shows itself in silence;
not in silence, but restraint."
Nor was he insincere in saying, "Make my house your inn."
Inns are not residences.

MARIANNE MOORE

THE SORROW

I folded his shirts with care
and emptied the nightstand drawer.
Given my sorrow's size,
I read Marguerite Duras,
hostile and saccharine Marguerite Duras,
who is knitting a shawl for her love.
On the fifth day
I opened the curtains.
Light fell on the greasy-stained bedspread,
the apartment full of trash,
the door frame peeling.
So much pain
from such ugly things.
I looked once more at his rat face
and threw all the trash in the garbage chute.
The neighbor
alarmed by how much I'd thrown away,
asked if I was doing all right.
It hurts, I told her.
In my mailbox, an anonymous note:
"One who has love
takes care
takes care
and does not clog the drain of the community."

MIYÓ VESTRINI

(TRANSLATED FROM THE SPANISH BY
ANNE BOYER AND CASSANDRA GILLIG)

from THE QUEST

IV

No window in his suburb lights that bedroom where
A little fever heard large afternoons at play:
His meadows multiply; that mill, though, is not there
Which went on grinding at the back of love all day.

Nor all his weeping ways through weary wastes have found
The castle where his Greater Hallows are interned;
For broken bridges halt him, and dark thickets round
Some ruin where an evil heritage was burned.

Could he forget a child's ambition to be old
And institutions where it learned to wash and lie,
He'd tell the truth for which he thinks himself too young,

That everywhere on his horizon, all the sky,
Is now, as always, only waiting to be told
To be his father's house and speak his mother tongue.

V

In villages from which their childhoods came
Seeking Necessity, they had been taught
Necessity by nature is the same
No matter how or by whom it be sought.

The city, though, assumed no such belief,
But welcomed each as if he came alone,
The nature of Necessity like grief
Exactly corresponding to his own.

And offered them so many, every one
Found some temptation fit to govern him,
And settled down to master the whole craft

Of being nobody; sat in the sun
During the lunch-hour round the fountain rim,
And watched the country kids arrive, and laughed.

W. H. AUDEN

THE DISPLACED OF CAPITAL

"A shift in the structure of experience . . . "
As I pass down Broadway this misty late-winter morning,
the city is ever alluring, but thousands of miles to the south
the subsistence farms of chickens, yams and guava
are bought by transnationals, burst into miles
of export tobacco and coffee; and now it seems the farmer
has left behind his plowed-under village for an illegal
partitioned attic in the outer boroughs. Perhaps
he's the hand that emerged with your change
from behind the glossies at the corner kiosk;
the displaced of capital have come to the capital.

The displaced of capital have come to the capital,
but sunlight steams the lingerie-shop windows, the coffee bar
has its door wedged open, and all I ask of the world
this morning is to pass down my avenue, find
a fresh-printed *Times* and an outside table;
and because I'm here in New York the paper tells me of here:
of the Nicaraguans, the shortage of journeyman-jobs, the ethnic
streetcorner job-markets where men wait all day but more likely the
        women
find work, in the new hotels or in the needle trades,
a shift in the structure of experience.

A shift in the structure of experience
told the farmer on his Andean plateau
"Your way of life is obsolescent."—But hasn't it always been so?
I inquire as my column spills from page one
to MONEY&BUSINESS. But no, it says here the displaced
stream now to tarpaper *favelas*, planetary barracks

with steep rents for paperless migrants, so that they
remit less to those obsolescent, starving
relatives on the *altiplano,* pushed up to ever thinner air and soil;
unnoticed, the narrative has altered.

Unnoticed, the narrative has altered,
but though the city's thus indecipherably orchestrated
by the evil empire, down to the very molecules in my brain
as I think I'm thinking, can I escape morning happiness,
or not savor our fabled "texture" of foreign
and native poverties? (A boy tied into greengrocer's apron,
unplaceable accent, brings out my coffee.) But, *no,* it says here
the old country's "de-developing" due to its mountainous
debt to the First World—that's Broadway, my cafe
and my table, so how can I today
warm myself at the sad heartening narrative of immigration?
Unnoticed, the narrative has altered,
the displaced of capital have come to the capital.

ANNE WINTERS

URGENT STORY

When the oracle said, "If you keep pigeons
you will never lose home," I kept pigeons.
They flicked their red eyes over me,
a deft trampling
of that humanly proud distance
by which remaining aloof
is its own fullness. I administered
crumbs, broke sky with them like breaking

the lemon-light of the soul's amnesia
for what it wants but will neither take
nor truly let go. How it revived me,
to release them! And at that moment of flight
to disavow the imprint, to tear
their compasses out by the roots of
some green meadow they might fly over
on the way to an immaculate freedom, meadow

in which a woman has taken off
her blouse, then taken off the man's flannel shirt
so their sky-drenched arc
of one, then the other above
each other's eyelids is a branding of daylight,
the interior of its black ambush
in which two joys lame the earth a while
with heat and cloudwork under wing-beats.

Then she was quiet with him. And he
with her. The world hummed
with crickets, with bees nudging the lupines.

It is like that when the earth counts
its riches—noisy with desire
even when desire has strengthened our bodies
and moved us into the soak of harmony.

Her nipples in sunlight have crossed his palm
wind-sweet with savor and the rest
is so knelt before
that when they stand upright
the flight-cloud of my tamed birds shapes an arm
too short for praise. Oracle, my dovecot
is an over and over nearer to myself
when its black eyes are empty.
But by nightfall I am dark
before dark if one bird is missing.

Dove that I lost from not caring enough,
Dove left open by love in a meadow,
Dove commanding me not to know
where it sank into the almost-night—for you
I will learn to play the concertina,
to write poems full of hateful jasmine and
longing, to keep the dead alive, to sicken
at the least separation.
Dove, for whose sake
I will never reach home.

TESS GALLAGHER

ST. ELIZABETH

I run high in my body
on the road toward sea.

I fall in love. The things
the wind is telling me.

The yellow sky quiet
in her quiet dress.

Old birds sending news
from the reddish hills.

& the one hawk flying
in the distance overhead.

That hawk is what
the wind says. In love

with the heaving
of my peacock chest,

with my lungs, two wings,
such flying things,

but mine for now, just for now
as I open my stride

above the good, dirt road,
fall in love with the mustard

& coriander dust,
& the far, far mountain

beveled by light, by rain,
the easy eye of the sun, now,

smoke floating across the hillside
like a face I knew once very well.

Very well, I fall in love
with the flowers & the wash

hung like prayer flags, see,
in red Juanita's yard. In love

with the earth the color of earth. In love
with the goats, their bellies & hooves,

& the goat mouths bleating
as they greet me on the road.

I fall in love. How they wear
their strange & double-eyes.

How they do not blink
or laugh at me

or say a thing I understand
when I ask them in my English,

because they circle around my feet,
as if they always *knew* me,

Were you my children once?
Did I know your names?

Oh, little magics?
Little children?

ARACELIS GIRMAY

GREENOCK AT NIGHT I FIND YOU

1

As for you loud Greenock long ropeworking
Hide and seeking rivetting town of my child
Hood, I know we think of us often mostly
At night. Have you ever desired me back
Into the set-in bed at the top of the land
In One Hope Street? I am myself lying
Half-asleep hearing the rivetting yards
And smelling the bone-works with no home
Work done for Cartsburn School in the morning.

At night. And here I am descending and
The welding lights in the shipyards flower blue
Under my hopeless eyelids as I lie
Sleeping conditioned to hide from happy.

2

So what did I do? I walked from Hope Street
Down Lyndoch Street between the night's words
To Cartsburn Street and got to the Cartsburn Vaults
With half an hour to go. See, I am back.

3

See, I am back. My father turned and I saw
He had the stick he cut in Sheelhill Glen.
Brigit was there and Hugh and double-breasted
Sam and Malcolm Mooney and Alastair Graham.
They all were there in the Cartsburn Vaults shining
To meet me but I was only remembered.

W. S. GRAHAM

I was born in Germany, in the fifties, to young and poor academic parents. They were in fact newly arrived Ossis, long before such a word existed. Both of them had starved during the war, they were conscientious, a little traditional (for want of anything else), remote from grandparents and advice, anxious to do well by their first child. My mother raised me on carrot juice (pressed with insistent effort through a piece of twisted muslin from carrots she had rasped herself) and (it appalls me to say so) shavings of raw horse's liver. The one was rich in vitamins, the other, dare I say it, in protein. I was, in the German sense of the word, a feisty child: firm-fleshed, with cheeks you could, like the breasts of some celebrated mistress or other, crack fleas on. My complexion glowed a healthy lunar orange from the carotene, or perhaps it was the horse. I talked and quipped and sang, and my besotted mother wrote it all down. Once, I was parked in my pushchair, in my favorite place on the veranda, which was at the head of the street and overseeing all of it, so that I could coo out my jocular commentary on whatever transpired there. My young and exuberant father (Kafka!) swung a bag of shopping over the parapet, tin cans, spuds, bottles, whatever, not knowing I was there; I took no harm. Nor from another occasion when I was found in the bathroom with an empty bottle of bleach and an ambiguous smile. Had I hadn't I? Who knows?

My earliest memory relates to food. I was four, in fact it was my fourth birthday, and I was allowed to go to the baker, all by myself, to buy fresh pretzels. No sooner, though, had I attained this level of perfect and infinitely auspicious competence than I was uprooted.

My father took a job—his first job—in England. We were emigrating.
I will have sensed the upheaval, the finiteness of things, so many
more times of this, three more times of that, the last time of any-
thing at all. I was solemnly presented with a pair of new shoes, "for
England," which I took and deposited in the stream at the bottom
of the garden (Freiburg, if you don't know it, is charmingly full of
flowing water). I don't know whether I was trying to save us trouble
and expense by allowing the shoes to go there under their own steam,
the way corpses, in the Jewish faith, go trundling along underseas to
Jerusalem—conceivably, I would have had some sense of rivers flow-
ing into each other, and then, along Father Rhine, and into the sea—
or if I was simply making my somewhat literal saboteur's protest.
My doubt, or equivocation, didn't save me. The shoes were expen-
sive. (Everything was expensive.) My father, a practical, hands-on,
and, truth to tell, irascible man, beat me. I was unable to expedite
the shoes or prevent our departure. We took our way from Freiburg
to Bristol. And then, on the boat, crossing the Channel, not in
England, nor in Germany, neither departed nor arriving, but extra-
territorially, in suspension, in no man's land, I had something in-
describably delicious to eat. I haven't the first idea what it was. I
don't know even whether it was warm or cold, here or there in its
inspiration, commercially wrapped or newly made. It was just "on
the boat," a prepositional phrase standing in for a noun. I have a
hunch it was savory rather than sweet, because that is where my
preferences lie; but for a child, even a child of the horse-and-carrot
variety, that seems a little unlikely. I think perhaps it was something

like Turkish delight, with its magical ingredient of rose water, but chances are it was more like beef jerky. At times, I have seemed close to remembering it. I may have seen it or known it in dreams. It was paradisiacally delectable, something experienced only by the barefoot in transit. Even its memory is fugitive. Perhaps it was my shoes.

MICHAEL HOFMANN, "DISORDER AND EARLY SORROW"

THOSE WINTER SUNDAYS

Sundays too my father got up early
and put his clothes on in the blueblack cold,
then with cracked hands that ached
from labor in the weekday weather made
banked fires blaze. No one ever thanked him.

I'd wake and hear the cold splintering, breaking.
When the rooms were warm, he'd call,
and slowly I would rise and dress,
fearing the chronic angers of that house,

Speaking indifferently to him,
who had driven out the cold
and polished my good shoes as well.
What did I know, what did I know
of love's austere and lonely offices?

ROBERT HAYDEN

THE CHURCH OF THE OPEN CRAYON BOX

Must be entered through the sharpener every Sunday,
else your name will be lovingly written in the Book
of the Down Arrow. The One Steeple to Every Church
                            rule breaks in half
in the Church of the Open Crayon Box; the One Bell
to Every Steeple rule breaks off its tip. "Climb stairs
to the steeples," the preacher commands, "and let
every belltone ring out!" You can see the whole town
        from the steeple, and you exit the church through
        the view, and you walk through what calls itself

                        Flagpole—the town is a blot
                    on the town, but the railroad
is coming out this way and we must give them a smear
to see through the windows: now you pass the General Store,
that even your vaguest stick figure can enter, now you pass
a vacant lot: the post office isn't here yet, is only a set-aside space
in the center of the country's envelope; now you pass the voting-
place, where we stuff our handwriting through a slit. Tall trees
fall in the pinewoods, tall telegraph poles are raised, and words
inch along our wires: text text text stop, text text text stop.

And now you pass the Feed Store, which sells carrot and turnip
and sugar-beet tops—only the visible parts—and now Whitey
BaLavender's Hardware, where everything hangs off the hook
of its color, or color hangs off the hook of its all, where you work
your hands into cool washers, and work hands into nailheads
of the color blue, and watch Whitey BaLavender busy himself
        pouring crayons into bullet molds. You show him a list
        that says "ax," and he sells you a red line through it.

All up and down Main Street ponies are covered
with strokes as coarse as horse blankets. And once
you have drawn the ponies you begin to draw the saddle
shop, you grip the right color like a saddle horn and somehow
keep from falling off, and you ride to the edge of town,
where you draw the fur trading post, where they sell tails
of any shy animal, the rest of the animal gone down a hole,
where you trade in your skin for a possibles bag and wear
possibles bag where your skin was. Fat geese fly in any letter
you like but you need red meat for once, and write a splayed-
hide word like "Deerslayer," and take hold of the ending
                                    and drag it home,

and now you are almost there, now you are building the home
with hand-drawn Log Cabin Font, you are building it log
by log of course and smoothing the logs with a color called
Adze, you are biting the crayon to notch the logs and driving
in dots of nailheads. Stumps of umber surround you, and the sky
is beginning to look like sky. You are hoping a man can be really
        alone here;
                you are hoping your father can tell what it is;
and now only the doorknob is left to draw and in your enthusiasm
you shout at the paper, and the weather
                changes just in time, not raining, beginning to spit.

PATRICIA LOCKWOOD

KITCHEN FABLE

The fork lived with the knife
     and found it hard—for years
took nicks and scratches,
     not to mention cuts.

She who took tedium by the ears:
     nonforthcoming pickles,
defiant stretched-out lettuce,
     sauce-gooed particles.

He who came down whack.
His conversation, even, edged.

Lying beside him in the drawer
     she formed a crazy patina.
The seasons stacked—
     melons, succeeded by cured pork.

He dulled; he was a dull knife,
while she was, after all, a fork.

ELEANOR ROSS TAYLOR

AT EIGHTY-THREE SHE LIVES ALONE

Enclosure, steam-heated; a trial casket.
You are here; your name on a postal box;
entrance into another place like vapor.
No one knows you. No one speaks to you.
All of their cocks stare down their pant legs
at the ground. Their cunts are blind. They
barely let you through the check-out line.
Have a nice day. Plastic or paper?

Are you origami? A paper folded swan,
like the ones you made when you were ten?
When you saw the constellations, lying
on your back in the wet grass,
the soapy pear blossoms drifting
and wasting, and those stars, the burned out ones
whose light was still coming in waves;
your body was too slight.
How could it hold such mass?
Still on your lips the taste of something.

All night you waited for morning, all morning
for afternoon, all afternoon for night;
and still the longing sings.
Oh, paper bird with folded wings.

RUTH STONE

There is a loneliness that can be rocked. Arms crossed, knees drawn up, holding, holding on, this motion, unlike a ship's, smooths and contains the rocker. It's an inside kind—wrapped tight like skin. Then there is the loneliness that roams. No rocking can hold it down. It is alive. On its own. A dry and spreading thing that makes the sound of one's own feet going seem to come from a far-off place.

TONI MORRISON, *Beloved*

FILLING STATION

Oh, but it is dirty!
—this little filling station,
oil-soaked, oil-permeated
to a disturbing, over-all
black translucency.
Be careful with that match!

Father wears a dirty,
oil-soaked monkey suit
that cuts him under the arms,
and several quick and saucy
and greasy sons assist him
(it's a family filling station),
all quite thoroughly dirty.

Do they live in the station?
It has a cement porch
behind the pumps, and on it
a set of crushed and grease-
impregnated wickerwork;
on the wicker sofa
a dirty dog, quite comfy.

Some comic books provide
the only note of color—
of certain color. They lie
upon a big dim doily
draping a taboret
(part of the set), beside
a big hirsute begonia.

Why the extraneous plant?
Why the taboret?
Why, oh why, the doily?
(Embroidered in daisy stitch
with marguerites, I think,
and heavy with gray crochet.)

Somebody embroidered the doily.
Somebody waters the plant,
or oils it, maybe. Somebody
arranges the rows of cans
so that they softly say:
ESSO—SO—SO—SO
to high-strung automobiles.
Somebody loves us all.

ELIZABETH BISHOP

QUESTION

Body my house
my horse my hound
what will I do
when you are fallen

Where will I sleep
How will I ride
What will I hunt

Where can I go
without my mount
all eager and quick
How will I know
in thicket ahead
is danger or treasure
when Body my good
bright dog is dead

How will it be
to lie in the sky
without roof or door
and wind for an eye

With cloud for shift
how will I hide?

MAY SWENSON

EDEN ROCK

They are waiting for me somewhere beyond Eden Rock:
My father, twenty-five, in the same suit
Of Genuine Irish Tweed, his terrier Jack
Still two years old and trembling at his feet.

My mother, twenty-three, in a sprigged dress
Drawn at the waist, ribbon in her straw hat,
Has spread the stiff white cloth over the grass.
Her hair, the colour of wheat, takes on the light.

She pours tea from a Thermos, the milk straight
From an old H.P. Sauce bottle, a screw
Of paper for a cork; slowly sets out
The same three plates, the tin cups painted blue.

The sky whitens as if lit by three suns.
My mother shades her eyes and looks my way
Over the drifted stream. My father spins
A stone along the water. Leisurely,

They beckon to me from the other bank.
I hear them call, "See where the stream-path is!
Crossing is not as hard as you might think."

I had not thought that it would be like this.

CHARLES CAUSLEY

WINDING UP

I live on the water,
alone. Without wife and children.
I have circled every possibility
to come to this:

a low house by grey water,
with windows always open
to the stale sea. We do not choose such things,

but we are what we have made.
We suffer, the years pass,
we shed freight but not our need

for encumbrances. Love is a stone
that settled on the seabed
under grey water. Now, I require nothing

from poetry but true feeling,
no pity, no fame, no healing. Silent wife,
we can sit watching grey water,

and in a life awash
with mediocrity and trash
live rock-like.

I shall unlearn feeling,
unlearn my gift. That is greater
and harder than what passes there for life.

DEREK WALCOTT

NURSING HOME

Ne tibi supersis:
don't outlive yourself,
panic, or break a hip
or spit purée at the staff
at the end of gender,
never a happy ender—

yet in the pastel light
of indoors, there is a lady
who has distilled to love
beyond the fall of memory.

She sits holding hands
with an ancient woman
who calls her *brother* and *George*
as bees summarise the garden.

LES MURRAY

from THE LIFE OF TOWNS

Apostle Town

After your death.
It was windy every day.
Every day.
Opposed us like a wall.
We went.
Shouting sideways at one another.
Along the road it was useless.
The spaces between.
Us got hard they are.
Empty spaces and yet they.
Are solid and black.
And grievous as gaps.
Between the teeth.
Of an old woman you.
Knew years ago.
When she was.
Beautiful the nerves pouring around in her like palace fire.

Death Town

This day whenever I pause.
Its noise.

Town of My Farewell to You

Look what a thousand blue thousand white.
Thousand blue thousand white thousand.
Blue thousand white thousand blue thousand.
White thousand blue wind today and two arms.
Blowing down the road.

ANNE CARSON

The Master-Maker in His making had made Old Death. Made him with big, soft feet and square toes. Made him with a face that reflects the face of all things, but neither changes itself, nor is mirrored anywhere. Made the body of Death out of infinite hunger. Made a weapon for his hand to satisfy his needs. This was the morning of the day of the beginning of things.

But Death had no home and he knew it at once.

"And where shall I dwell in my dwelling?" Old Death asked, for he was already old when he was made.

"You shall build you a place close to the living, get far out of the sight of eyes. Wherever there is a building, there you have your platform that comprehends the four roads of the winds. For your hunger, I give you the first and last taste of all things."

We had been born, so Death had had his first taste of us. We had built things, so he had his platform in our yard.

And now, Death stirred from his platform in his secret place in our yard, and came inside the house.

ZORA NEALE HURSTON, *Dust Tracks on a Road*

BOOK ENDS

I

Baked the day she suddenly dropped dead
we chew it slowly that last apple pie.

Shocked into sleeplessness you're scared of bed.
We never could talk much, and now don't try.

You're like book ends, the pair of you, she'd say,
Hog that grate, say nothing, sit, sleep, stare . . .

The "scholar" me, you, worn out on poor pay,
only our silence made us seem a pair.

Not as good for staring in, blue gas,
too regular each bud, each yellow spike.

A night you need my company to pass
and she not here to tell us we're alike!

Your life's all shattered into smithereens.

Back in our silences and sullen looks,
for all the Scotch we drink, what's still between 's
not the thirty or so years, but books, books, books.

II

The stone's too full. The wording must be terse.
There's scarcely room to carve the FLORENCE on it—

Come on, it's not as if we're wanting verse.
It's not as if we're wanting a whole sonnet!

After tumblers of neat *Johnny Walker*
(I think that both of us we're on our third)
you said you'd always been a clumsy talker
and couldn't find another, shorter word
for "beloved" or for "wife" in the inscription,
but not too clumsy that you can't still cut:

You're supposed to be the bright boy at description
and you can't tell them what the fuck to put!

I've got to find the right words on my own.

I've got the envelope that he'd been scrawling,
mis-spelt, mawkish, stylistically appalling
but I can't squeeze more love into their stone.

TONY HARRISON

THE SOLITARY LAND

I inhabit these fugitive words,
I live, my face my face's lone companion,
And my face is my path,

In your name, my land
That stands tall, enchanted and solitary;
In your name, death, my friend.

ADONIS

(TRANSLATED FROM THE ARABIC BY

KAREEM JAMES ABU-ZEID AND IVAN EUBANKS)

I began to watch places with an interest so exact it might have been memory. There was that street corner, with the small newsagent which sold copies of the *Irish Independent* and honeycomb toffee in summer. I could imagine myself there, a child of nine, buying peppermints and walking back down by the canal, the lock brown and splintered as ever, and boys diving from it.

It became a powerful impulse, a slow intense reconstruction of a childhood which never happened. A fragrance or a trick of light was enough. Or a house I entered which I wanted not just to appreciate but to remember, and then I would begin.

EAVAN BOLAND, *Object Lessons:*
The Life of the Woman and the Poet in Our Time

from ANNA LIFFEY

In the end
It will not matter
That I was a woman. I am sure of it.
The body is a source. Nothing more.
There is a time for it. There is a certainty
About the way it seeks its own dissolution.
Consider rivers.
They are always en route to
Their own nothingness. From the first moment
They are going home. And so
When language cannot do it for us,
Cannot make us know love will not diminish us,
There are these phrases
Of the ocean
To console us.
Particular and unafraid of their completion.
In the end
Everything that burdened and distinguished me
Will be lost in this:
I was a voice.

EAVAN BOLAND

BLACK MAP

In the end, cold crows piece together
the night: a black map
I've come home—the way back
longer than the wrong road
long as a life

bring the heart of winter
when spring water and horse pills
become the words of night
when memory barks
a rainbow haunts the black market

my father's life-spark small as a pea
I am his echo
turning the corner of encounters
a former lover hides in a wind
swirling with letters

Beijing, let me
toast your lamplights
let my white hair lead
the way through the black map
as though a storm were taking you to fly

I wait in line until the small window
shuts: O the bright moon
I go home—reunions
are one less
fewer than goodbyes

BEI DAO

(TRANSLATED FROM THE CHINESE
BY ELIOT WEINBERGER)

—No one lives in the house anymore—you tell me—; all have gone.
The living room, the bedroom, the patio, are deserted. No one
remains any longer, since everyone has departed.

And I say to you: When someone leaves, someone remains. The
point through which a man passed, is no longer empty. The only
place that is empty, with human solitude, is that through which no
man has passed. New houses are deader than old ones, for their
walls are of stone or steel, but not of men. A house comes into the
world, not when people finish building it, but when they begin to
inhabit it. A house lives only off men, like a tomb. Except that the
house is nourished by the life of man, while the tomb is nourished
by the death of man. That is why the first is standing, while the
second is laid out.

CÉSAR VALLEJO, Human Poems

THESE

are the desolate, dark weeks
when nature in its barrenness
equals the stupidity of man.

The year plunges into night
and the heart plunges
lower than night

to an empty, windswept place
without sun, stars or moon
but a peculiar light as of thought

that spins a dark fire—
whirling upon itself until,
in the cold, it kindles

to make a man aware of nothing
that he knows, not loneliness
itself—Not a ghost but

would be embraced—emptiness,
despair—(They
whine and whistle) among

the flashes and booms of war;
houses of whose rooms
the cold is greater than can be thought,

the people gone that we loved,
the beds lying empty, the couches
damp, the chairs unused—

Hide it away somewhere
out of the mind, let it get roots
and grow, unrelated to jealous

ears and eyes—for itself.
In this mine they come to dig—all.
Is this the counterfoil to sweetest

music? The source of poetry that
seeing the clock stopped, says,
The clock has stopped

that ticked yesterday so well?
and hears the sound of lakewater
splashing—that is now stone.

WILLIAM CARLOS WILLIAMS

In every poet there is a loss or an absence. In every poet there is an Andalus. Otherwise how do we interpret the sadness of poetry and its thrust into two contradictory directions: the past and the future. And poetry is the search for an Andalus that is possible to recall, able to be presenced. From here grows the mysterious happiness, not in reality, but from creation, when the words are able to capture the impossible.

MAHMOUD DARWISH, *Crypts, Andalusia, Desert*

All I know about music is that not many people ever really hear it. And even then, on the rare occasions when something opens within, and the music enters, what we mainly hear, or hear corroborated, are personal, private, vanishing evocations. But the man who creates the music is hearing something else, is dealing with the roar rising from the void and imposing order on it as it hits the air. What is evoked in him, then, is of another order, more terrible because it has no words, and triumphant, too, for that same reason. And his triumph, when he triumphs, is ours.

JAMES BALDWIN, "SONNY'S BLUES"

from BLUES

Trane

Propped against the crowded bar
he pours into the curved and silver horn
his old unhappy longing for a home

the dancers twist and turn
he leans and wishes he could burn
his memories to ashes like some old notorious emperor

of rome. but no stars blazed across the sky when he was born
no wise men found his hovel; this crowded bar
where dancers twist and turn.

holds all the fame and recognition he will ever earn
on earth or heaven, he leans against the bar
and pours his old unhappy longing in the saxophone

Bass

Bassey the bassist
loves his lady

hugs her to him
like a baby

plucks her
chucks her

makes her
boom

waltz or tango
bop or shango

watch them walk
or do the 'dango:

bassey and his lovely lady

bassey and his lovely lady
like the light and not the shady:

bit by boom
they build from duty

humming strings and throbbing
beauty:

beat by boom
they build this beauty:

bassey and his lovely lady

KAMAU BRATHWAITE

from ON R.L.S. AND HAPPINESS

I know the motions of the horses—
The motions of faith—and it is time
That I insist, even though the Jew

Couldn't prove he was human. Neither
Can you. I can't prove the horse, but here
Is your pain anyway, and here are

Instructions against it. It's a salt.
Consider the ocean. Consider
The infinite fishes, how they swim.

Consider us at shore, weeping
To show our sympathy with water.
It's not enough. Only in the most

Careful details of the most extreme
Philosophies, the most careful stones
Of the breathless cathedrals, the claims

Of the most elaborate musics
On our souls do we start to dissolve
As though we had a home, and lived there.

VICKI HEARNE

FOR HAROLD BLOOM

I went to the summit and stood in the high nakedness:
the wind tore about this
way and that in confusion and its speech could not
get through to me nor could I address it:
still I said as if to the alien in myself
    I do not speak to the wind now:
for having been brought this far by nature I have been
brought out of nature
and nothing here shows me the image of myself:
for the word *tree* I have been shown a tree
and for the word *rock* I have been shown a rock
for stream, for cloud, for star
this place has provided firm implication and answering
    but where here is the image for *longing:*
so I touched the rocks, their interesting crusts:
I flaked the bark of stunt-fir:
I looked into space and into the sun
and nothing answered my word *longing:*
    goodbye, I said, goodbye, nature so grand and
reticent, your tongues are healed up into their own
element
and as you have shut up you have shut me out: I am
as foreign here as if I had landed, a visitor:
so I went back down and gathered mud
and with my hands made an image for *longing:*
    I took the image to the summit: first
I set it here, on the top rock, but it completed
nothing: then I set it there among the tiny firs
but it would not fit:
so I returned to the city and built a house to set

the image in
and men came into my house and said
    that is an image for *longing*
and nothing will ever be the same again

A. R. AMMONS

Already the Great Khan was leafing through his atlas, over the maps of the cities that menace in nightmares and maledictions: Enoch, Babylon, Yahooland, Butua, Brave New World.

He said: "It is all useless, if the last landing place can only be the infernal city, and it is there that, in ever-narrowing circles, the current is drawing us."

And Polo said: "The inferno of the living is not something that will be; if there is one, it is what is already here, the inferno where we live every day, that we form by being together. There are two ways to escape suffering it. The first is easy for many: accept the inferno and become such a part of it that you can no longer see it. The second is risky and demands constant vigilance and apprehension: seek and learn to recognize who and what, in the midst of the inferno, are not inferno, then make them endure, give them space."

ITALO CALVINO, Invisible Cities

MID-AUGUST AT SOURDOUGH MOUNTAIN LOOKOUT

Down valley a smoke haze
Three days heat, after five days rain
Pitch glows on the fir-cones
Across rocks and meadows
Swarms of new flies.

I cannot remember things I once read
A few friends, but they are in cities.
Drinking cold snow-water from a tin cup
Looking down for miles
Through high still air.

GARY SNYDER

ACKNOWLEDGMENTS

I am very grateful to the following:

Christian Detisch, whose intelligence and alacrity have been indispensable at every stage of this book.

Jennifer Banks, my editor at Yale University Press, who helped conceive *Home* over coffee one pre-Covid afternoon in downtown New Haven, and who also allowed me to smuggle one extra poem into this book when I couldn't bear to let any of them go.

Martin Jean and the Yale Institute of Sacred Music, who provided additional financial support for the publication of this book.

CREDITS

Every effort has been made to obtain all necessary permissions for copyright-protected work. If you believe your copyright-protected work was included in this publication without necessary permission, please contact Yale University Press.

"If China," by Stanisław Barańczak, from *Selected Poems: The Weight of the Body,* trans. Magnus J. Krynski (Evanston, IL: TriQuarterly Books, Northwestern University Press, 1989). © 1989 by Stanisław Barańczak. All rights reserved.

"We Will Rise," by Sophia de Mello Breyner Andresen. © Richard Zenith.

"Home," by Andrea Cohen, from *Everything.* Copyright © 2017 by Andrea Cohen. Reprinted with the permission of The Permissions Company, LLC on behalf of Four Way Books, fourwaybooks.com.

"Nostos," by Louise Glück, from *Meadowlands.* Copyright © 1996 by Louise Glück. Used by permission of HarperCollins Publishers, and by kind permission of Carcanet Press, Manchester, UK.

"Ode: Intimations of Immortality," by William Wordsworth, from *Poems, in Two Volumes,* 1807.

from *The Niagara River,* by Kay Ryan, copyright © 2005 by Kay Ryan. Used by permission of Grove/Atlantic, Inc. Any third party use of this material, outside of this publication, is prohibited.

from "On R.L.S. and Happiness," by Vicki Hearne, from *Tricks of the Light,* University of Chicago Press. © 2007 by The Estate of Vicki Hearne. All rights reserved.

"Trane" and "Bass," by Kamau Brathwaite, from "Blues," in *Other Exiles,* Oxford University Press, 1975. © 1975 Kamau Brathwaite.

from *A Timbered Choir: The Sabbath Poems, 1979–1997,* by Wendell Berry. Copyright © 1998 by Wendell Berry. Reprinted by permission of Counterpoint Press.